Mono
Diggings

FRANK S WEDERTZ

Historical Sketches of Old Bridgeport
Big Meadows and Vicinity
Copiously Illustrated

Wedertz, Frank S.
    Mono diggings.
    Bibliography: p.
    Includes index.
        1.   Mono Co., Calif.—History.   2.   Mono Co., Calif.—
Biography.   I.   Title.
F868.M67W43   979.4'48'00992   78-1839
ISBN 0-912494-28-X
ISBN 0-912494-29-8 pbk.

Sketches and map
    W. Lee Symmonds
Book design and graphics
    Russ Johnson and Georgia Summers
Printed and distributed by
    Chalfant Press, Inc., Bishop, CA 93514

This book
is
dedicated
to
M. A. "Slick" Bryant

Contents

Preface

There is much in Mono County history that is not covered here. The Antelope Valley and Benton areas are rich in history yet to be collected. The Mono Indians and Piutes would alone be the subject for lengthy work. Little has appearaed concerning the natural and earth history of the area. All is future work and is here for those interested.

I have included several lengthy biographies, those of R. G. Watkins and R. M. Folger, for the purposes of illustrating how personal histories and county histories relate to the entire history of the State and the West and to illustrate the adventures of those who followed the rush to the gold discoveries of 1849. The County is unique in having had almost every major explorer cross through it.

I thank those families who have preserved their histories and shared their records and pictures with us. I thank the pioneer journalists who knowingly and unwittingly recorded what they saw and heard. No attempt has been made to cover "everything", additional materials, pictures, names and descendants appear and surface almost daily.

I thank the following for help in this works Alice Dolan, Grace Crocker, Wes Berreyesa, J. Brandon and family, County Assessor Dan. Bryant and staff, County Clerk Ann Webb, Art Webb, Mono County Historian Lee Symmonds, M. A. Bryant. The Nevada State Historical Society furnished copies of the Whitney letters. I especially thank my wife, Roberta, and my father, Gilbert, for helping with this. Many of the photographs here are reproduced from original glass plates taken by pioneer photographer Joshua West Towle between 1878 and 1906.

Frank S. Wedertz

A Mono Chronology of Events

1827—Jedediah Strong Smith party crosses the Sierra.

1833—Joseph R. Walker Party crosses the Sierra.

1841—The Bidwell-Bartleson Party; the first successful emigrant crossing of the Sierra.

1844—John Charles Fremont Party crosses the Sierra.

1852—Lieutenant Tredwell Moore's Indian-fighting expedition crosses the Sierra to Mono Lake via Bloody Canyon and exhibited promising ore samples upon their return to Mariposa.

1852-53—The Lee Vining Party crosses to Mono Lake Basin via Bloody Canyon. Possibly the first quartz location-1854.

1857—The Walker River placers of Dogtown attract attention. Col. Moorman is there.

1859—Cord Norst discovers the Monoville placers. The rush to the Mono Diggings has begun.

1859—The Bodie deposit is discovered in the Fall.

1860—The Aurora-Esmeralda mines are discovered in the summer. The Masonic District is discovered and organized.

1861—The Esmeralda District and Aurora become the population center.

1861—Mono County is created; the County Seat is set at Aurora.

1863—The September election brings about the removal of the County Seat to Bridgeport. The Montgomery Mining District near Benton is organized.

1865—The town of Benton is now the largest in the County in terms of population.

1868—Sonora-Mono Wagon Road is in passable condition.

1872—Owens Valley Earthquake shakes Bridgeport.

1877—The Bodie boom begins. Lake District (Mammoth) organized. Heavy activity has occurred at the Dunderberg mines.

1878—Tioga District, near Tioga Lake, organized. First and only legal infliction of the death penalty in Mono Co.

1879—Bloody Canyon mines became part of the Prescott District. Homer Mining District (Lundy) organized.
Keith Mining District near Moorman Meadows is organized.
Jordan Mining District on Copper Mountain is organized.

1879-82—Bodie at its peak in population and production.

1880—Patterson Mining District formed in the Sweetwater Mtns. The first issue of the **Bridgeport Union** appears.

1881—Bridgeport Courthouse is built. DeRoche is executed by vigilantes at Bodie. Bodie-Mono Mills railroad is built.

1882—Bodie begins to show signs of a decline in production and population as several large mines close.

1883-84—Lundy crime reaches its peak. The County begins to enter an economic depression; the Bodie mines have failed.

1890's—The Dunderberg mines show promise.

1892—Fire destroys most of the town of Bodie. The world's first hydroelectric transmission plant sends electricity produced at the Green Creek Dynamo to the Standard Con. Mine at Bodie: steam power is replaced.

1895—The cyanide process revives the Bodie and Lundy mines.

1900—The Masonic mines show great promise.

1908—Fire destroys a portion of Bridgeport.

1911—Heavy storms result in several deaths.

The Naming of Mono

Mono County took its name from that strange lake whose salt waters and desolate volcanic surroundings fascinated its first Indian and white visitors—the latter, especially Zenas Leonard and Mark Twain, noting that the caustic quality of the water was strong enough to cure a coyote hide. The lake was, in turn, named for the tribe of Indians inhabiting its shores and nearby foothills; they too felt the mystery, and the lake, with its contrasting black and white islands, was central to their myths and rituals. From the inception of the county, however, the meaning of the word "mono" was lost in a confusion of definitions to the extent that Spanish, Greek, and Latin etymologies were resorted to in order to produce such fitting, so they felt, definitions as "alone", "desolate", and "beautiful". The problem as to what "mono" exactly meant resulted in a good deal of controversey as this anecdote printed in the *American Flag* of 1864 relates:

In the winter of 1860, a man and a wife, and half a dozen others remained in Monoville with the intention of wintering there. They were all that were left of the large population of miners that had worked that season. The wife gave birth to a boy and everything passed off as well as could be expected under the primitive circumstances. The male population all manifested a lively interest in the youngster, it being the firstborn of Monoville. A self-constituted committee held a meeting and took immediate measures to name the child. The matters were quickly concluded and the committee, with all the pomp and circumstance of the occasion, marched into the presence of the new mother, and, through their chairman, announced that the meeting was over and the child's name was Mono. The chairman congratulated the mother and remarked that the name was not alone beautiful, but very appropriate. At this moment a Pike County bull-driver, who was in town for a load of lumber, and had entered the dwelling to warm himself, spoke up and said: "See here, Misses, I consider this—yes, I'm blowed if it ain't—I would not stand it, no how; these

11

*fellers think as how they're mighty smart, and have a
heap of larnin'; and I'll be goldarned if they haven't
called the sweet little 'un of yourn a—yes, a monkey!"*
That destroyed the committee and they fled from the
angry mother.

The above revealed yet another erroneous definition of the
word "mono", which some obviously felt was related to the Spanish
word for monkey. The name "mono" was eventually traced by
Kroeber to the Yaquis of the western slope of the Sierra Nevada,
in whose language it meant fly or flies. Kroeber, unable to make
any real connection between the Yaqui definition and the Mono
Indians, neglected to consider, noted anthropologist that he was,
that a tribe was often named for what was most unusual or unique
about it, and this case was unique indeed. The Yaqui term referred
to the Mono's chief nourishment, which was unusual, and which
was noted by every observant traveler who passed by Mono Lake.

The Monos, or Monachi, were known as the fly-people because they harvested the small larvae of the Ephydna-hyana, which
inhabited the briny lake water. This larvae the Monos called Ko-
cha-bee, and when it washed ashore, usually in enormous quantities,
the larvae was scooped up in winnowing baskets, dried in the sun,
the shell rubbed off, and then packed away for winter use. The
yellowish kernel that remained was about the size of a grain of
rice and was, as Henry De Groot and William Brewer noted, very
nutritious and not unpleasant in taste. It was this larvae that sus-
tained members of the Joseph R. Walker party in their October
1833 crossing of the Sierra.

When the larvae washed ashore, swarms of flies gathered
around the masses, and, to other Indians, it appeared as though
the Monos were eating flies; hence the naming of the Monos, the
Monachi, the fly-people. As late as July of 1883, the *Reno Evening
Gazette* reported that the surface of Mono Lake was covered with
flies and that Indians were harvesting. As the Indian population
disappeared through disease and assimilation with the whites, so
did this curious habit of the "fly-people."

Trappers, Explorers and Emigrants

JEDEDIAH STRONG SMITH

In a note, whose authenticity is its face value, Robert Lyon reported that Rocky Mountain Jack and Bill Reed, who were at the Mono Diggings in 1860 and were fur trappers, had been members of the Jedediah Strong Smith party.[1] The Smith group was the first white group crossing the Sierra, and in Smith's return crossing, from west to east, estimates of what his route may have been range from Donner Pass to the Kings Canyon. He began the crossing on May 20, 1827, and the Robert Lyon note states that, once they had crossed over the Sierra, both Rocky Mountain Jack and Bill Reed recalled spending a week in prospecting and picking up gold in the foothills around Mono Lake; the latter is valuable information in regard to where Smith may have emerged from the eight-day crossing through snow four to eight feet deep. They lost two horses and one mule, small losses in comparison to hardships suffered by later trappers, explorers, and emigrants.

Further confirmation as to the whereabouts of the Smith expedition appears in a letter written in 1860 by Thomas Sprague in which he states that gold was found on the route to Salt Lake, headquarters of the fur company, east by north of Mono Lake.[2]

1. Thompson and West, *History of Nevada,* p. 21. The only question of authenticity raised seems to be one of date as the note cites 1825 rather than 1827.
2. Bancroft, *California Inter Pocula.* As Bancroft notes, the Sprague letter is only partially correct.

13

Winter scenes of old Bridgeport town. To the far left can be seen a windmill, erected by Frank L. Wedertz. Note the huge winter supply of pine nut cord wood. The last highway bridge on the old crossing stands out well. The viewer is looking west from across the East Walker. A second scene shows a heavy snow on Main in front of the old Allen Stables and granary and a mountain clipper freight wagon. A third, looking southwest, shows a small residence on the corner of School and Main and the Schoolhouse in the distance. The last photo, taken from near the present airport, shows the back of the Allen House, the larger building on the left; the front of the old Leavitt stables, and the Courthouse. One can imagine, in seeing this snow load at 6,500 feet, what Fremont and others encountered as they forced across the Sierra.

14

JOSEPH REDDEFORD WALKER

In addition to the first white men to have crossed the Sierra, came Walker and the first winter crossing, Fremont and Kit Carson, and the first emigrant train to California, all struggling through the rugged terrain of what is now Mono County. Walker had learned of Smith's successful expedition, and, through Smith and the fur company, had probably been told of a route. Setting out from Salt Lake on a fur trapping expedition, the Walker expedition of 50 mounted men, horses, supplies, and ammunition reached, via the Humboldt, the eastern base of the Sierra near Bridgeport. It was fall of 1833, and before Walker was through crossing the Sierra he and his men had dined on seventeen horses, all butchered to feed the famished party.

From clerk and fur trapper Zenas Leonard, a member who left a chronicle of the expedition, we have accurate information as to parts of the route. Leonard noted that on the evening of October 10, 1833, the party camped near the edge of a large lake which had no outlet and was formed by a river which headed in the mountains. Leonard, like Mark Twain and many others who followed thirty years later, remarked that the lake water was similar to lye and tasted much like pearl-ash and that its waters were useful in washing clothes as no soap was needed.[1] This, to those familiar with the area, is a very accurate description of Mono Lake. "There is also a great quantity of pumice stone floating on the surface of the water, and the nearby shore is covered with them."[2] The nearby Mono Craters could have produced the pumice, Leonard noted, but it is very likely that he mistook the calcareous tufa formations, which rise from the lake bottom, and the white-stained country rock, for pumice. Even competent geologists have so mistaken the white rock, stained by the heavily saline lake waters. Leonard's account seems to place the party at Mono Lake.

The next day was spent in following the river, which fed the lake, towards the mountains, where they again camped for the night; snow extended halfway down the mountains, and the expedition was almost out of dried buffalo meat. Provisions were now very short, and a colt was killed for meat. Then, in scouting

15

ahead for a pass, Walker, George Nidever, and Leonard moved into steep ground and heavy timber. Nidever, who had become separated from the others, was startled to see two Indians running near him. He shot them both with the same shot, supposing that they had caused trouble with Walker and Leonard. Much to his dismay, Nidever soon discovered that the Indians had been scared; Leonard noted several times that Nidever was very upset about having killed them, and this was probably the first disastrous encounter between whites and Indians in the Mono region. It is likely that the party scouted the eastern scarp of the Sierra, between what is now known as June Lake and Green Creek, in search of a pass.

Soon they discovered some Indian trails, one of which had recently been traveled by horses. The most heavily traveled Indian routes were through Bloody Canyon, Virginia Lakes Canyon, and Green Lakes Canyon. Bloody Canyon is by far the most natural pass and was one of the most heavily used, but either of the three would have led them to the edge of towering precipices where they became the first whites to almost literally fall into the Yosemite.[3]

On October the 16th, six days after leaving the lake and before reaching what is thought to be the Yosemite, Leonard stated that they had not yet reached the top of the mountains. They may, however, have reached the crest of the Sierra without realizing it since the Sierra consists of several series of peaks, descending slowly to the west but dropping abruptly along the eastern scarp. Even at Tuolumne Meadows, for example, the uninitiated explorer might assume that he had not yet reached the top because of the broad western extent of mountainous country when, in fact, if he had known of the Indian trails he would have known that he was over the crest and on his way into the Yosemite. Such were the circumstances, however, that made for exploring, and for quick and sometimes irrational decisions as to routes.

Now they encountered rocky and steep ground; there was nothing for the horses to eat and snow was deep. The party fed on juniper berries and insects from the lake, the food having been given to them by Indians.[4] Men and horses made only eight to ten miles per day in breaking road through the heavy snow. There was now a desperate struggle to survive and some of the party threatened mutiny; they were feeding on butchered horses. After five days, the explorers scared an Indian; the men feasted on the acorns he had dropped and knew they were close to warmer climates. Soon they were past the Yosemite and into the San Joaquin, another "successful" crossing of the Mono Sierra.

1. Leonard, *Adventures of Zenas Leonard, Fur Trader,* p. 73.
2. Ibid., p. 74
3. Early Mono county news accounts note that in the fall it was a common practice for Indians to cross the Sierra to gather acorns. Former Chief Jack Lundy recalled crossing via Green Lakes Canyon when a boy.
4. This would be the larvae harvested by the Monos at Mono Lake and would be another piece of evidence to place the party at Mono Lake before its crossing.

JOHN CHARLES FREMONT: EXPLORER-AGENT

Mono County history is rich in lore concerning the second expedition of John Charles Fremont. In 1894, for example, a pair of deer horns was brought to Carson City from Antelope Valley. The block of the tree that had grown around the horns was cut twelve feet from the ground. The prongs, which protruded from the bark, were quite a curio and were shipped to San Francisco to be exhibited at the Midwinter Fair.[1] The embedded horns, found in Lost Canyon, were, in 1895, decorating the Bridgeport saloon of F. M. Richardson.[2]

In regard to the fabled howitzer, which the Fremont party had carried to Oregon to be finally abandoned somewhere between what is now Virginia City and Alpine County, W. P. Merrill had found a cannon ball near the line between Mono and Alpine counties and had given it to Judge Arnot of Alpine County. It too was exhibited in San Francisco before being forwarded to Jessie Benton, Fremont's wife.[3]

Perhaps the most unusual of Fremont stories appeared in the Bodie *Daily Free Press* in 1882.[4] There, in Lost Canyon, it was claimed, Fremont cached a portion of his artillery, and there three of the men who perished on that trip were rolled into blankets and buried. Midway up the canyon stood the butt of an old pine, and, on the side of the tree, was a partially destroyed inscription which had been carved in the bark: James Mat-Aug. 184-. Under those letters were the remains of others. A second article appeared in which men stated that they had been scared off, after being bedded down in Lost Canyon, by an apparition in military uniform riding a horse.[5]

The motives behind Fremont's second expedition remain unclear as he was definitely not scouting trapping ground. He headed an exploring party and carried a howitzer. The United States was continuing to expand, knowing that Mexico and England still claimed territorial rights to the Pacific Coast. His second expedition may be evaluated in light of the results of his third expedition, which was central to the conquest of California.[6]

Fremont, a lieutenant in the United States Topographical Engineers, was the son-in-law of influential Missouri Senator Thomas Hart Benton. Fremont was put in charge of an expedition consisting of 39 men: Preuss, topographical engineer; Thomas Fitzpatrick, guide; Theodore Talbot and Frederick Dwight; a free

Negro, Jacob Dodson; Kit Carson and Alexis Godey, guides; and two Delaware Indians were among the party. They left Kansas in May of 1843, reached the Hudson Bay Company outpost on the Columbia, in Oregon Territory, and from there, in late November, moved south. The trip was to consume eight months. On January 22, 1844, Fremont noted that they were flanking south along the eastern base of the Sierra, following two streams; Indians carried pinenuts in small bags. On the 25th at two below zero, Fremont noted volcanic mountains at the 38th parallel; the estimated elevation was 6,300 feet. On the 29th the howitzer was abandoned; Indians told them of a good pass farther south and of twelve men who crossed nearby about two years earlier.[7] A desperate need for food and animals, however, led Fremont to strike directly across the Sierra in January, 1844.

As to the Fremont route across the Sierra, it is generally believed that he followed either the West or East branches of the Walker River; the latter Eastern fork is a less likely route, but Fremont's notes indicate that he camped in what is now Bridgeport Valley. In following the Eastern fork of the Walker, Fremont left the river at a point near the old Nine Mile Ranch, in what is now Nevada, crossed behind Masonic Mountain by following a well-defined Indian trail and natural pass paralleling Rough Creek, which took the expedition through the Half Way Flats and then west into Bridgeport Valley. There in Bridgeport Valley, the expedition camped at the junction of Robinson, Swauger, Buckeye, and the East Walker River, a point now under the present Bridgeport Lake. The next day the party traveled to the point where Swauger Creek emerges from its canyon.[8]

The Swauger Creek campsite has long been pointed out by pioneers of Mono as the Fremont Camp, and, in his notes, Fremont remarked that, after leaving camp, they came upon a hot spring, seeing the steam rising over the ridge. Some of the men were quite upset that they had not camped there, at what is now Fales Hot Springs. The expedition was following very close to the present route of Highway 395, northwest of Bridgeport, along what placer miners later described as a very well marked Indian trail which led from Leavitt Meadows to Bridgeport Valley. Once, however, in the area between Leavitt Meadows and Antelope Valley, it is obvious that Fremont was lost.[9]

As the expedition attacked the eastern wall of the Sierra, against the advice of nearby Indians, men and animals worked to

19

beat down a trail through heavy snow six feet deep on the level. They were reduced to eating mule meat while the surviving mules ate leather and each others tails. The expedition, fortunate to not have met the fate that the Donner Party suffered, arrived at Sutter's Fort on March 8, 1844, almost eleven months having passed in the most rugged trip from Kansas.[10]

1. *Bridgeport Chronicle-Union*, 2/17/94.
2. *Bridgeport Chronicle-Union*, 2/7/95.
3. At the request of the then sheriff, F. L. Wedertz was hired to look after a band of lost sheep in Lost Canyon. He found much debris there indicating either emigrants or explorers had passed. He recalled seeing howitzer type balls at the head of Leavitt Meadows.
4. Bodie *Daily Free Press*, 9/19/82.
5. While in Lost Canyon, F. L. Wedertz saw the graves noted.
6. The mythical Buenaventura River, which was thought to flow from the Rockies to the Pacific, was the public motive for much of Fremont's initial work; this is now discounted as a motive by many who feel that acquisition of California was the prime one.
7. John C. Fremont, *Memoirs of My Life*.
8. Most physical evidence shows that Fremont passed through Bridgeport Valley, camped at the mouth of Swauger Canyon, and saw Fales Hot Springs the next morning. This is the alternative to the theory that he traveled up the West Walker through Antelope Valley. At any rate, the party was lost once it struck into the Sierra.
9. It is doubtful that the party was lost enough to retrace 26 miles north through the Sierra.
10. Carter, *Dear Old Kit*.

BIDWELL-BARTLESON: EMIGRANTS OF 1841

The Bidwell-Bartleson Party, which preceded Fremont's second expedition by three years, formed in Kansas Territory in late 1840 and materialized into an actual movement west as Bidwell and a few determined pioneers set out in complete ignorance of any route to California, Bidwell stating that he only knew that California lay west. As emigrants joined along the way, the party soon consisted of sixty-nine men, women, and children. Jack Bartleson was, according to Bidwell's narrative, chosen Captain because he brought seven or eight men and because he wanted to be. The teams were of oxen, mules, and horses. A guide, Captain Fitzpatrick, led them from Kansas around the north end of Salt Lake until the Bear River was struck, and a portion of the group went to Fort Hall. The main party was eventually reduced to thirty-two when half decided to go with Fitzpatrick north into Oregon Territory. Bidwell and the rest resolved to go on directly to California, and, in so doing, became the first emigrant train to successfully cross the Great Basin and the Sierra.

A great deal of time was consumed in making road for the wagons, and there was trouble in finding water. The only directions given the party were to not go too far north or too far south. Indians were a constant concern. Upon reaching the Humboldt River, many had left their wagons and were on foot; by the time they had struggled to the Sink of the Humboldt, half the weary party was on foot, and supplies were packed on oxen and mules. Near the Humboldt Mountains, Bartleson and his men left the slow moving party, feeling that they could get to California more quickly.

After leaving the Sink of the Humboldt, the emigrants crossed a large stream which Bidwell later believed was the Carson River and moved on to the Walker River, following it up to where it emerged from the Sierra. They were now camped on the Walker River at the very eastern base of the Sierra where they were joined by the Bartleson group, which had circled farther south. In Bidwell's words: "We ascended the mountains on the north side of Walker River to the summit, and then struck a stream running west, which proved to be the extreme source of the Stanislaus

21

River. We followed it down for several days and finally came to where a branch ran into it, each forming a canyon."[1]

The emigrants picked their way up and down canyons, forcing the animals up by pulling and pushing them, the men often carrying the packs of animals. Oxen, crow, and wild-cat formed their diet as they pushed through the high Sierra wilderness. Most of the animals were finally left behind and were cut up for meat by Indians. When the emigrants eventually reached the edge of the San Joaquin Valley, they were strung out and each slept where darkness overtook him.

It was now about the first of November, and many of the party, totally without bearings, still felt that they were some five hundred miles from California. Soon they stumbled into Dr. Marsh's Ranch near Mt. Diablo. "After six months we had arrived at the first settlement in California, November 4, 1841."[2]

1. John Bidwell, "First Emigrant Train to California."
2. Ibid.

EMIGRANTS

In the names of Fremont Lake, Emigrant Lake, and Upper and Lower Relief Camps, are recorded the memories of the explorers and emigrants who, after the discovery of gold in California, crossed through Mono County via the West Walker River, Leavitt Meadows, and close to what is now Sonora Pass. One party, who had left its wagons behind in an ascent of the Sierran eastern wall, dropped over the crest and sent men on ahead, hoping that they would return with supplies and aid for the party. The advance party did return to save the emigrants at what are now the Relief Camps.[1]

The Cherokee, or Trahern Party, moving west, attacked the Sierra from Leavitt Meadows and formed the first oxen train over the Sonora route. The Duckwells, members of the party, had two large ox-drawn wagons and six children. There were others, including a number of Cherokees, who had traveled over 1500 miles, led by George Washington Trahern. Included among the large number of ox teams were five hundred cattle. The ascent to the crest was torture. Wagons were pushed, pulled, lifted with rope and block and tackle anchored to trees and rock up and down and across the steep granite crest. As many as six oxen were hitched behind wagons to act as brakes. Two wagons were completely wrecked before the party reached Relief Camp on September 27, 1853.[2] Such were the adventures of explorers and emigrants through Mono prior to the rush of 1857-60 which took them back across the Sierra in search of gold on the eastern slope. Prospectors, attracted to the Mono Diggings, commented with wonder at the wreckage, the rope burns cut through pine and juniper, and the skeletons of animals that litered the emigrant route from Sonora to Leavitt Meadows.

1. Buckbee, *The Saga of Old Tuolumne,* pp. 395-96.
2. Ibid., pp. 397-98.

Early Placer Mining: Dogtown and Monoville

In 1859 about 150 people wintered at Monoville, and some suffered considerably because of a great blizzard which began on the 16th of November and did not stop until the snow was five feet deep. One man, W. S. Bodey, discoverer and namesake of the nearby Bodie mines, was frozen to death while attempting to reach Monoville. Provisions, which had become scarce, had to be brought from Genoa, ninety miles north of Monoville. The successful return of the provisions to the young camp was made, and the men and the heavily laden sleds thus averted a disaster that would have, perhaps, surpassed that suffered by the starving Donner Party. A man named Lamb who hiked to Genoa with W. W. Vaughn had both feet frozen.[1] Vaughn reported that, in mid-December, the snow was three feet deep at Monoville, and miners were being forced to leave because of the intolerable living conditions. Ninety miles from any settlement in California or Nevada Territory, at the very eastern base of the Sierra, several miles away from running streams, miles away from trees, overlooking the heavily saline waters of Mono Lake, an unusual setting for placer mining—an unusual setting for living in 1859. A notation in the ledger of Sierra packer J. M. Luther, listed "cast-steel-soap", an accidental reflection of the conditions in Mono.[2]

Life in the Monoville placer mining camp was rugged. The working season was, at its very best, eight months; then heavy snow forced a close and many miners crossed the Sierra back to settlements in Mariposa, Kern, Tulare, Fresno, Calaveras, and Tuolumne counties, and other settlements to the West. Walker's Pass, much further south than Bloody Canyon, Sonora Pass, or the Placerville route, was a favorable winter crossing. In addition to the extreme winter conditions, the cost of living at Monoville was three times that of any other place in California.

The first placer settlement was at Dogtown, seven miles south of Bridgeport, on a branch of the Walker now known as Dogtown Creek. The actual date of discovery and settlement has not yet surfaced, but as early as June of 1853, the *Sonora Herald* mentioned Walker River and Carson Valley, suggested that the best route was via Sonora Pass and that a good mule could travel it in two days.[3] The LeRoy Vining Party was in the area in the early 1850's, as was Col. Thomas J. Moorman. Col. Moorman gave his name to the nearby Mormon Meadows and Ranch, later cartographers and historians having confused his name with that of the Mormon movement.[4] The rush to Carson Valley and Washoe overshadowed the Mono excitement and the prospecting being done on what then was called Brown's Creek, suggested another discoverer's name. Cord Norst, who remained at the diggings for many years, and who discovered the Mono Diggings at what became Monoville, stepped forward and stated that he had also discovered the Dogtown deposit.

The Dogtown gold seems to have accumulated in placer deposits, perhaps both pre-and post-glacial, from auriferous dikes and veins on Dunderberg Mountain and Slope, from where the waters of Dogtown Creek head. Dogtown, as the name suggests, never produced much in comparison to the fabulous placer deposits of the western Sierra slope, even though a $50 nugget was reportedly discovered there.[†]

From Dogtown, however, the placer excitement moved south with the discovery, on July 5, 1859, of the Mono Diggings by Cord Norst.[5] The Mono placer period of 1859-60 was distinct from both the Washoe and later Esmeralda excitements, the latter depopulating Monoville, Bodie, and the new Masonic District; yet, however, they were almost simultaneous events.

In the spring of 1859 Josiah Kirlew and about five others left Sacramento with a pack train bound for the Washoe excitement, but at Virginia City they separated and Kirlew and a young man named Oliver left for Dogtown Creek. They crossed Big Meadows (Bridgeport Valley) and ascended Dog Creek, prospecting, and stopped at the house of a white man who had a Chinese wife.[6] Another curiousity at Dogtown was a small store kept by a French-woman, a widow. A report from 1861 noted that she was supposedly a "doctoress" and was, at that time, married. Upon surveying the scene at Dogtown, Kirlew found that almost all had left for the Mono diggings, so Kirlew and Oliver pushed on over the present Conway Summit area to Monoville, as the diggings came to be called.

There they found Lee and Dick Vining, Joshua A. Talbot, Jim Dods, Cross (a cripple), Ramsey, and others from Toulumne and Mariposa counties all engaged in mining.[6] Kirlew and Oliver

† Supervisor William Wetherill showed the nugget in 1881, the largest reportedly taken on the eastern slope.

began mining for wages, but when their employer cleaned up he skipped the camp and carried all his dust with him. Meanwhile, the two had located a claim which they considered valuable, but Oliver became discouraged and exchanged his interest in the claim for Kirlew's pack animal.

While Kirlew was still at Monoville, a man named Farnsworth came in on horseback, showed a bullet mark in his leggings, and said that his partner had been killed by Indians while crossing the Owens River. The miners doubted the story but did not suspect Farnsworth of murder. Shortly afterward some men came in and reported having found the headless body of a man on an island at the crossing of Owens River, but they reported that the Indians everywhere were peaceable.[7] Lee Vining observed that Farnsworth's leggings were powder-burnt, as though he himself had fired the shot at close range. These circumstances led the miners to call a meeting, place Farnsworth under guard, and send a committee to Owens River to investigate the matter. The committee of nine went to an Indian camp near the scene of the murder and explained the matter to the chief, and the latter, with a squad of warriors, accompanied the committee to where the body had been buried, exhumed it, and held an inquest.

One of the Indians said that two white men had been camped on the river about three miles above where the body had been found. The committee went to the camp, and they found everything covered with blood, although an attempt had been made to cover the area with bushes. Leading from the camp to a cliff overhanging the river, they found the blood spots on the granite and noted that an effort had been made to obliterate them by the use of charcoal. The head of the murdered man, with a hatchet wound on the right side, was found among some roots at the edge of the river.[8]

The committee took the head and started back to Monoville, first dispatching two men post haste to inform the miners of what had been discovered and to tell them to put Farnsworth in irons. The night before these two men reached Monoville, Farnsworth escaped during a snowstorm. He was never recaptured. The murdered man was named Hume and came from San Francisco. Farnsworth had met him at Virginia City and said that he had a very rich claim on the Owens River, which he would sell cheaply, and induced Hume to go. Hume had a fine gold watch and $700 in gold which Farnsworth took. Kirlew afterwards met Farnsworth on the Umatilla River in Oregon; the former had sold his claim at Monoville, drifted on to prospect at Bodie, later returning to see ground he had once located yielding thousands of dollars to the owners.

Another Monoville arrival in the spring of 1859 was R. K. Colcord, who crossed the Sierra via the old emigrant trail from Columbia. His partners were Abe Black, Bill Stevens, and George Smart. Colcord, who later followed the Esmeralda excitement to Aurora, subsequently became governor of Nevada. About 70 men had preceded the Colcord party to the Mono Diggings, and he had known two or three of them while on the western slope. Sol Carter, a trans-Sierra packer; ex-Senator W. W. Williams, later a wealthy Nevada stockman; and Teddy Brodigan, father of a later California Secretary of State. Another, Frank Shaw, became a cattleman in the Benton area. He had been a gentleman gambler in Columbia and had, in Monoville, the only sizeable tent, where he was dealing monte and taking bets in gold dust.

Colcord found that there was little water with which to carry on sluicing and rocker operations after September; a few had made money while the spring runoff water could be trapped and used to wash gold. Nearly everyone, he reported, left before the storms set in, and passed through Big Meadows en route to the western slope. He returned the following summer but passed on to the Esmeralda-Aurora strike.

The 1859-60 season was the peak of the Monoville rush; the camp population swelled that summer to well over 500. Some estimated that there were fully 900 people but few wintered there. The post office, established on December 12, 1859, was closed on April 4, 1862.[9]

Billy Milliken, who also arrived in 1859, kept a large two-story building there. The first floor was used for drinking, gambling, and general hilarity, and the second story was rented as lodging space. A restaurant was also attached, and he made gold dust so fast he had to keep a barrel under the counter. In those days, Milliken recalled, the keeping of a saloon or gambling house in the town of Mono required a good deal more courage, caution, and vigilance than was required of one tending a Sunday school.

Milliken noted that Dick Vining, Jim Dods, and others were handy with guns, and old Tat Tatman, a gentleman from Missouri who represented Mariposa County in the Assembly of 1857 was also there and was known for swinging a 16-inch bowie knife with his four foot arm. But the greatest danger Milliken encountered was that of the threat of being talked to death any evening by Josh Talbot, the first State Printer of Mississippi, formerly a lieutenant of the United States Navy, and a captain of volunteers in Mexico, subsequently an officer in the Mexican Army, which subdued the natives of Yucatan, and one of two men who fitted out a $50,000 expedition to explore and prospect the then unknown headwaters of the Amazon River. He was one of the most interesting conversationalists living, and also a versatile writer. He worked his jaw in Mono Diggings all the summer of 1859; then footed it to Genoa and worked on the *Territorial Enterprise* for his board. Talbot, who was mining recorder of Mono District, afterwards went to Arizona where he "died". He wrote a lengthy obituary, more than a column in length, and then showed up in Los Angeles.

There were others of note, such as Dan De Quille, who visited the camp in 1859 while collecting material for stories. Some, like John Carlin, accumulated a modest stake that enabled them to establish businesses or ranches elsewhere, Carlin having gone into ranching in Lyon County, Nevada. James Sinnamon, for whom the extensive Sinnamon Cut at the Diggings was named, did well enough at placer mining to purchase prime ranch land in Bridgeport Valley, where he was well established in 1873. For references to others, consult the First Directory of Mono Residents,

As a result of very promising prospects found at the Monoville placers, a stampede was well underway by the early spring of 1860. One popular route was via Keysville and the South Fork of the Kern River. Droves of cattle and hogs were readied and many companies, with from one to two wagons apiece, were readied at Visalia, loaded with such necessities as flour, bacon, whisky, mining tools, and billiard tables. One company, composed of N. A. Hicks and E. W. Heath, left Visalia with 2,500 pounds of provisions and was back for more within a month to stock their new trading post at Monoville. The trip from Keysville to Monoville was made via the Owens River and took at least thirteen days.

One company from Martinez was of special interest as it was headed by none other than explorer and trapper Joseph R. Walker, who was now nearly 70 and planned to take his 13-man party across Walker's Pass. They left Visalia in March, heading for territory that Walker had not seen since 1833.

Other parties from Big Oak Flat and Butte County also passed through Visalia, but reports from the Mono Diggings varied from the wildly enthusiastic to the most pessimistic and discouraging. The excitement reminded pioneers of the frenzy of '49 and many hoped for a placer bonanza equal to that of the fabulously rich western Sierra.

By late April of 1860 almost all the ground around Mono Lake had been staked off, and the gold was what miners called shot gold, not very coarse but easily recovered in placering and worth $14 - $15 per ounce. A town was laid out and hotels, stores, and saloons were rapidly being added to the settlement of '59. Mail arrived weekly from Genoa. Timber was plentiful on the Sierra slopes to the west and three sawmills had already been erected; a fourth was under construction on the south side of Mono Lake. Lumber was $70 per thousand feet. Talbot, district recorder, warned that there was not vacant ground enough with water facilities, necessary for gold placering, for more than two hundred men. He had been there eighteen months and warned men not to come to Mono.

Estimates as to the population of the camp varied from 500 to 2000. There was trouble over claim jumping and water rights; several small ditches were under construction. A man from Greenhorn named Farant had paid $4,000 for a claim in the fall and had cleared it, besides his water and grub, in twenty-six days. The price of flour had dropped from $50 to $18, and bacon and sugar were forty to fifty cents per pound. Town lots sold from $50 to $300 and often doubled in value over night. Charles B. Smith, of Visalia, built the first house in Monoville. He reported that about eight streams from spring run-off ran through the diggings and there had been several fights.

But not everyone who visited Monoville saw the same things:

Placerville, 5/30/60

J. E. Denny, esq.:

I have been to Mono Lake, Walker's River, and to the Silver Mines, and nothing I find but snow, cold weather, and crazy men. There is no use talking, the American people are crazy sure. There is in the Silver Mines some ten thousand men—they would look more like an ant bed to you than anything else, running in every direction, hunting for something they don't know what . . . I think a merchant could do well at Mono Lake, though it will not pay many of them. Water

29

scarce—I saw all the Visalia boys but Hicks, and left them all carrying sagebrush to burn to keep from freezing to death. Orrick sends his respects to you all, he was nearly naked when I saw him. Tell the boys to stay at home for I think the excitement is about played out. I left Bartlett and Lawrence at Mono short of grub and not a cent, and no work to be got. When I left Mono, flour was 30c a pound, whisky $2.00 per bottle, and tobacco $2.00 per pound—everything else in proportion, though these were the staple articles.

R. C. Proctor[10]

Another, in June noted that he could make only $2.00 per day. But it was the usual story, the rich diggings were confined to a small area, and facilities for working were poor. Some claims were very rich and paid one pound of gold per day to the hand. Ten pounds of gold was taken from the claim of Ramsey and Bradley and Co. in eighteen hours of washing. In general, however, the placers were not paying as well as miners expected.

By late July of 1860, Monoville consisted of about forty houses, some of them two stories.† Twenty-two of them were saloons, and there were two bottle hotels, two blacksmith shops, two butcher shops, two launderies, one hospital, and all kinds of gambling and games. James McFarlan had started an express from Mono to Sonora, for papers, letters, and packages. William Grey started an express from Coultersville to Mono. Money was short and many disappointed men were leaving. Hundreds would have left if they could but they were waiting to make the four days grub necessary to take them over the Sierra.

It was now obvious that if the placer mines were to be developed, an adequate water supply must be provided, as Colcord and others had noted. The Monoville, or Mono, placers were situated in dry gulches and ravines amid huge weathered granite boulders and pinnacles, just to the east of present Highway 395 at the southern base of Conway Summit. Through erosion, gold had weathered out of small crevice veins and accumulated in gravel deposits in the dry gulches and ravines, the only water being available during the spring. Some men packed dirt on their backs from claims three-quarters of a mile away from the nearest water. Therefore, much of the summer of 1860 was devoted to the construction of extensive water ditches, one of which, when completed, was felt by historian Bancroft and others to have been one of the greatest pieces of work ever accomplished in any portion of California;

30

† The main portion was in Rattlesnake Gulch, Bacon and Spring Gulches also were populated.

the remoteness and working conditions added to the unusual nature of the accomplishment. When completed, its cost was estimated to have been $75,000. On October 20, 1860, overjoyed miners learned that water was in the ditch, and one of the most difficult of tasks undertaken in the State had been concluded.

The ditching project was begun in June of 1860 when a company of 300 was formed, by selling shares at $50 each for the purpose of construction of the ditch, which was estimated to be fourteen miles long. The United Water Ditch Company was under the supervision of R. M. Wilson[11] and two hundred men were put to work. The ditch commenced at the east fork of Walker River, or Vaughn's Creek as it was then known, and thence down the south side of the river three miles to Dogtown Creek, thence southwest five miles to Virginia Creek, thence east around present Conway Summit[12] to Monoville. The ditch was to deliver 1,100 inches of water; they had to whipsaw 40,000 feet of lumber to complete the ditch and the large flume which crossed east over Conway Summit; at an elevation of over 8,000 feet above sea level, whipsawing was no easy job. With water in the ditch on October 20th, the camp was alive with trading and selling. Another ditch, known as The Old Mono Ditch, headed at the mouth of Mill Creek Canyon, and skirted the eastern base of the Sierra north to Monoville. This ditch was owned by Cross and Company. The ditches were to figure directly in the later history of the camp; whoever controlled the ditches controlled the placer mining.

Aside from the ditch construction, the October correspondence from Monoville of 1860 was largely confined to the marital problems of Mr. Watts, whose wife had abandoned him for a man named Donaldson. In fact, in late September, Mrs. Watts had informed her husband that she was leaving and taking all their money with her. Mr. Watts appealed to the miners to make her return it. She did, and Mr. Watts then made her a present of $90 in gold, a bag of silver, and a wagon and team. The miners again assembled and made Donaldson treat the whole camp to drinks; during the course of the festivities Donaldson made a speech in which he accused Mr. Watts of counseling him to take the course he had.

The correspondent relating the Watts' news was impressed with the miners' diet of eggs, which were gathered on the two islands in Mono Lake and sold in the camp. Then, like many others, on the way back west from Monoville the correspondent

31

almost perished in a snowstorm and ran out of food. He met a man named Underwood and both feasted on the carcass of a deer that had been killed by a bear.

Considerable snow had fallen in Monoville and many feared for their safety. A packer who had attempted to cross the Sierra to the camp was forced to turn back; and neither of the steady packers, Sol Carter, nor McQuade, had been heard from. In February of '61 Mono was sarcastically described as "a pleasant place" with five to eight feet of snow on the ground. Captain Vining's saloon yielded to the pressure and caved in; another's residence was lost under a 25 foot drift. Watts' long lost wife had repented and returned, and, in another jibe, the correspondent noted that "the times are prolific with Union troubles." Most Visalians had already left Mono by mid-November, 1860, avoiding the heavy winter described above. A. H. Mitchell, Mayfield, Smith, and Talbert were busy in Visalia describing how miners in Mono had averaged $10 per day to the hand, a larger average, they claimed, than could be boasted of anywhere else in California.[13]

In the early spring of 1861, the water companies were ready to furnish water to the placer miners at 25c an inch, but a note dated July 4th stated that the ditches were still frozen and money was scarce. Miners were doing nothing. The creation of Mono County and the June election of County Officers had taken place but not without some Union and Secessionist conflict, which resulted in the formation of a Monoville Union Club in August headed by Captain William Cobean Meredith and boasting a membership of 143.[14] Monoville, the major polling place for the June election, recorded almost 500 names, but many were now residents of the other nearby mining areas.[15]

During the summer of 1861, trading was brisk in Monoville, although it had not yet been determined whether the camp was in California or Nevada Territory. Allen and Henderson's Saloon, on the north side of Main Street, was worth $1,500, big money for a townsite that today defies detection by most who have been to the gulches. Opposite Vaughn's Restaurant on Main Street was a frame store and dwelling. East of this was a livery stable and to the west was Levy's house. Safford and C. W. Mills' Bowling Saloon was on the east side of Main, joined Allen and Henderson's Saloon on the north, and had two ten-pin alleys in the bar. It was opposite the stable of Jones & Co.

The photograph shows Henry Donnel and wife Louisa Wedertz. Henry's almost fatal crossing of the Sierra to Monoville must have resulted in eventual success as he settled comfortably at Bridgeport near the present site of Ken's Sporting Goods. The Donnel residence led to the site becoming known as the Donnel corner. Upon his death in 1886 at age 56, the Ohio native left a wife and three daughters. Ella, while still quite young, worked the case on the CHRONICLE-UNION, and the Folger brothers called her their angel. Two other daughters, Addie and Clara married into local families, the Kirkwoods and Murpheys. This photograph was taken in the early 1870's at Iowa when the Donnels accompanied L. E. Wedertz to Germany and Holland to investigate a family inheritance. On the return trip, an attempt was made to assassinate L. E. Wedertz at sea.

The boarding house of Humprey, Shed & Co., who operated a sawmill near Monoville, was located on Main between a blacksmith shop and the residence of Dr. Gills. William Boatright and J. A. Shreve owned a saloon and blacksmith shop there.

On High Street was the American Bakery, which was owned by A. W. Luckett and John Miller. The Rialto Saloon, which was just south of the shoe store of A. Fanman, had been owned by H. Kiethly, E. Dunham, and A. Mack and was on the west side of High Street. The Tulare Hotel, owned by William T. Hanford, and H. A. McGaffey and the store of P. S. Labatoure were other fixtures of High Street.[16]

The Miners' Market, Lamb & George Smith's Market, and Timmons Saloon were other Monoville establishments. On the east side of Mono Gulch was a five-room boarding house, which boasted a front balcony, three bedsteads, three tables, two gaming tables, and eight benches, all that was left when the property sold.

33

A one-third interest in the 1,200 foot placer mining claim, flume, sluices, tools, and cabin of Wm. Williamson, J. W. Gunn and B. W. Harwood, brought a price of $1,400. It was located in Long Gulch. Other claims along Mono and Bacon gulches were also being sold or traded.

1861 had brought its usual influx of spring arrivals, two of whom had a narrow escape in crossing the Sierra by the Coulterville trail. Z. B. Tinkum and Donnel[17] traveled together until they arrived at the forks of the Cascade on the Tuolumne where Donnel fell behind and missed Tinkum's trail. Donnel, snowblind, was rescued by Indians and taken to Murphey's Camp and, although he had been without food for three days, recovered and was soon back on the trail. The snow was deep and Tinkum barely escaped; it took him several days to cross. He too ran out of food and was forced to sample his supply of soap before reaching Monoville. Both later settled in Bridgeport.

T. N. Machin, who was elected to the California State Assembly from Mono in 1861 and who was elected Lieutenant Governor of California in 1863, found that his law practice at Monoville afforded him a rare opportunity for studying rough characters and fun. On one occasion two justices of the peace and two constables were elected; none of them ever gave bonds or qualified in any way, yet went ahead and did business, the lawyers and people standing in accordingly.

One of the justices, Luckett, kept his docket in his head, and the other, Brown, could not read or write. There was a tall serious-faced attorney from Ohio named Phelps, who dressed in summer in a very long duster and who was given to make the best of the two courts. He referred to Luckett's as the court above because of its location on a hill looking down on Brown, whom Luckett held in violent contempt. Brown, on the other hand, was terrified of Luckett. In one mining case, Luckett was called as a witness in Brown's court, but instead of being on time, hid in the sagebrush. Bob Lowden, a long-haired, wild-eyed constable, dragged him in. Another witness named Williams rode a mule into the courtroom, gave his testimony, and rode out without dismounting. In the meantime, Cherokee Liz, who weighed three hundred pounds, came in screaming and asking for legal protection. She had just been nearly scalped by a blow from a six-shooter, and, Machin noted, the blood streamed down in streaks over her otherwise clean white dress giving her the appearance of the rebel flag and Southern Confederacy struck by lightning.

During these highjinks, Machin claimed, there were over 1,000 men at Monoville; there were only three women. The first to arrive was a Negro woman from Visalia. Machin does not mention Watts' wife, and perhaps she was gone. The second woman was called Kit Carson, and was the daughter of the famous explorer who had passed through Mono County years before. Her name was really Adaline Carson. In 1853 she had married Louis Simmons and had left for California with her father. Fur trapper Simmons apparently left her and she later married George Stilts, or Stiles.[18] It was thought that she died near Mono Lake in 1860, but the date is in error as on January 20, 1862, Adaline Carson appears in Mono County Clerk Records as receiving $100 from B. F. Snyder at Aurora.[19] She was, however, buried near the old Wilson Ranch at Mono Lake. The last of the trio was Cherokee Liz.

Once, Machin continued, it was reported that the stone house people, as the Owensville community near Bishop was known, were surrounded by hostile Indians. About forty men from Monoville saddled up and got as far as what is now known as the Goat Ranch, where they camped for the night. Finding in the morning that their supplies, almost entirely whisky, were short, they sent back for more, and in the end the stone house had to take care of itself. Such fun was common practice and, during one Sunday celebration, a purse of $25 was given to a Negro man who rode a bucking horse.

Like many others, Machin prospected from his base camp at Monoville, and once, while prospecting in the Owens River area, he and a companion were stopped by Indians, who took their guns and horses. They were made to walk back home, which, Machin stated, they were very glad to do.

In June of 1862, only about 150-200 men were at Monoville, the previous summer rush to the Esmeralda District having depopulated the camp. It had snowed on May 25th and the wind was blowing hard. Supplies were still expensive: "When a man gets hungry or ragged he must wait a month or three weeks until what he wants can be brought from Placerville." (letter dated June 1, 1862). Since whoever controlled the water held the future of the camp, there were many organizations and reorganizations of the major ditches. In 1863, for example, the old ditch from Virginia Creek to Monoville became the Lake Water Co., and was owned by Judge H. Keever, R. Stadtz, H. Lewis, A Thompson, and William Cross. These men were not now miners themselves, and others soon became discouraged with water politics. In the September election of 1865, Mono Precinct polled only 27 votes. In 1871 John Till acquired the old Mono Ditch, formerly owned by Cross and Co., and the ditch from Mill Creek, with all flumes, dams, and reservoirs. When Till sold the property the following year, to Patterson and Barnes, it included all hydraulic hoses and pipes used by Gunn and Sinnamon in Mono and Bacon gulches.

Dogtown, whose placer deposits were not extensive, was gradually abandoned to the Chinese, who, for the next decade, cleverly gleaned what little gold was left behind. In the late 1860's, over twenty Chinese occupied the ground, and one ran a small store. Le Conte, who passed through Dogtown in the early

Pioneer miner of Monoville, James Sinnamon, shown here on his favorite horse. Sinnamon was at Monoville prior to 1861 and did very well in mining at what has become the Sinnamon Cut, an extensive hydraulic mining cut still visible a few miles east of the southern base of Conway Summit. Sinnamon Meadows, on Dunderberg Slope, bears the pioneer's name. Sinnamon went into ranching at Big Meadows. Sinnamon married Mattie Obenchain in 1879 who was a daughter of rancher and lumberman T. J. Obenchain.

36

John C. McTarnahan left Louisville, Kentucky, in February of 1850 at the age of 26. He crossed the plains with an ox team and arrived at Nevada City September 5th of that year. He was a surveyor and helped build several railroads in the state. At one time railroads interests were directed to Mono County when the mines appeared to make the construction of a railroad a possibility. McTarnahan came as agent and stayed to placer mine at Dogtown. He later became a mail carrier and made several remarkable snowshoe trips through blizzards from Bridgeport to Bodie and back. They were tremendous feats of endurance. He died at Sonora in 1895.

1870's, noted that the little stone huts and cabins of the Chinese each had a small green garden in front. The Chinese, excluded by the whites, were allowed to work over abandoned ground. Then, in 1878, probably as an offshoot of the Bodie excitement, interest in the Dogtown placers was renewed, large claims were taken, and ditches were dug to reach higher ground. Several thousand acres were patented. Working the old ground about this time was J. C. McTarnahan, who built an extensive sluice down the canyon. Attempts to rework the Dogtown placers were not very profitable in outcome, if there was any profit at all. Several old stone cabins remain near the grave of Peter Anderson above the gravel mounds left by dredging operations of the 1900's.

William Cobean Meredith, born in 1817 in Pennsylvania, kept the notes of the Monoville Union Club in 1861. He died at Duarte in 1917. A brother, James M. Meredith, crossed the plains in 1849 and arrived at Sacramento where he spent two years and then returned to Pennsylvania. In 1852 he again came overland and in 1854 was City Marshal at Sonora. In 1860 he came to the Mono Placers. He moved on to Aurora where he ran a merchantile business and was postmaster there. Other members of the Monoville Union Club included D. Francis, who was Governor of Missouri, and, in 1896, was appointed Secretary of the Interior. It was noted that he was a friend of J. W. Towle and P. G. Hughes of Bridgeport. Barna Mc-Kenna, who died in 1880, became Superintendent of Mono County Highways. A curiosity from the list of Members of the Monoville Union Club is the name of J. F. Finney, known as "Old Virginia", and for whom Virginia City, Nevada, was named. He apparently died in 1862.

Meanwhile, at Monoville, where many still feel good placer ground exists, Louis Lockberg was, in 1878, investing money he had made at the Bodie strike and had taken a placer claim of 5,000 feet, had the necessary water power, and had constructed about a mile and one half of sluices. He died, however, just before his plans were completed, and John W. Stewart of Bridgeport took over.

In 1881 Stewart was getting ready to hydraulic mine on a large scale. On the ground was ¼ mile of six-inch pipe, 10,000 feet of lumber for sluices, and ten men were put to work. The ground reportedly payed .02-.03c per pan in gold. Stewart's death in 1883 put an end to the operation, which was known as the Squawvine and was located a short distance southwest of the Sinnamon Cut.[20]

The settlement of Monoville was quite important as the camp had served as the locus from which prospectors, roaming in all directions, made discoveries which were to form the economic-political base for the formation of the present County. The Bridgeport Valley settlement, ranches, and nearby sawmills were directly connected to the needs of the nearby mining camps, and the economy fluctuated in response to the lives of the mining camps. Miners from Monoville discovered and established, in 1859, the Bodie District; in 1860, the Esmeralda District, Masonic, and Benton districts were discovered and soon were attracting the population that was to form early Mono County.

1. *Territorial Enterprise,* 12/17/59.
2. "Day Book of J. M. Luther," Oct. 25, 1861.
3. *Sonora Herald,* 6/11/53.
4. Leroy Vining, so spelled in the 1861 Mono Precinct Poll list and Col. Thomas Jefferson Moorman were early arrivals. Maule reports that Leory Vining came to California in 1852 and was a native of La Porte, Indiana. Vining's Ranch was on Vining's Creek (S ½, Sec. 4, T. No. 1, R. 26E), and on July 9, 1861, he sold it to Lewis Van Reed (Book A, Deeds, p. 130, Mono County Clerk's Office). Moorman owned what is now called the Morman Ranch; he owned other property, but is listed in Mono County Great Registers of 1880-82 as a miner, aged 70, a native of North Carolina. He apparently was not successful financially, and there is probably at least a family connection between him and Madison Berryman Moorman (see *Journal of Madison Berryman Moorman*).
5. Cord Norst is given credit, largely through his own efforts to do so, for both the Dogtown and Monoville placer discoveries.
6. Nat Luce, J. F. and H. H. Dods, and Talbot appear in numerous accounts and records.
7. This often misquoted story has become part of the lore of the Lost Cement Mine.

8. Some reported that the head was kept at Monoville, pickled in a barrel as a curiosity.
9. Frickstad.
10. *Visalia Weekly Delta,* 5/12/60.
11. R. M. Wilson was among the first at Monoville.
12. This was a hand dug double ditch system. Ditch No. 1, for example, began from a point on the west fork of Dogtown Creek known as Thompson's Camp (Thompson's wood camp was high on the slope of Dunderberg, the remains of the camp and ditch are still quite visible). The creek was damned; after 1864 the flumes broke down and the ditches filled in. The total length of the double system was about twenty-eight miles, the ditches being quite visible today as parallel contours around the present Conway Summit.
13. *Visalia Weekly Delta,* 11/17/60.
14. See Appendix for Monoville Union Club material.
15. See Appendix for list.
16. W. T. Hanford has probably a connection with the town of Hanford, Calif.
17. Z. B. Tinkum later held Mono County office. See Tinkum biographical data.
18. Carter, *Dear Old Kit.*
19. Mono County Records: Adaline Carson Stiles, Book A, p. 307.
20. The depth of the placer ground is indicated in a cut made by Taylor and Stewart in 1881 in which a gravel bank twenty feet high was exposed above the bedrock. Seventeen feet of it was considered paydirt. Some tunneling was done and some arrastras were operated.

Mono County Organized

"We have just organized our county and think we have a pretty fair set of officers—they can all drink plenty of whisky—but whether they can steal or not remains to be seen, and that is the necessary qualification for a California officer." Correspondence dated Monoville, June 19, 1861; Visalia Weekly Delta, 7/4/61.

The rush to Dogtown and Monoville in the late 1850's was closely followed by the discovery of rich gold and silver deposits at Bodie, Masonic, and Aurora. Those from California who arrived in the Mono and Esmeralda Districts found themselves separated from their established seats of justice and government by the most imposing of natural barriers, the massive eastern wall of the Sierra Nevada, which, when winter struck, was literally impassable, impregnable.

By December of 1860 an application had been drawn to be presented to the California State Legislature for the organization of a new county out of the country known as the Mono and Esmeralda districts. Almost eight hundred people had been there that summer, and about three hundred intended to winter there. Citizens of Mariposa, Tulare, Fresno, and Calaveras counties had petitioned for the creation of a "Mono" county. In the form of a bill, and a different label, "Esmeralda" county, the need was again presented. Action on the bill was taken, not after what appears to be an unusual length of time considering the mineral wealth involved, and the name "Mono" was settled on.

On April 24, 1861, the creation of Mono County, out of those portions of Calaveras, Mariposa, and Fresno counties lying east of the summit of the Sierra Nevada Mountains and north of the southern boundary line of Fresno County, was approved as an Act and signed by the Secretary of The State of California on May 10, 1861. The seat of justice was set at Aurora; an election was to be held June 1st, 1861, to elect county officers.

Other forces, also noting the wealth of the gold and silver of Mono and Esmeralda districts, acted more swiftly than had California, and on March 2, 1861, the Territory of Nevada was organized by an Act of Congress; the new governor, James Nye, named Aurora as one of the election districts and Esmeralda as

41

one of the nine counties of the Territory. Both California and Nevada Territory now claimed the same country which lay along the as yet imaginary, unsurveyed boundary between the two, Aurora serving as the seat of justice for both Esmeralda and Mono counties. Thus the stage was set for a two-year territorial, jurisdictional, and governmental contest that, because of the then current national civil struggle and the acquisition of allies by northern and southern factions, focused on the valuable mineral deposits and was not resolved until September of 1863.

In June of 1861 there were 1400 people at Esmeralda (Aurora) and about seven hundred at Monoville; the need for laws and local justice for the protection of life and property was becoming acute. Monoville property owners, for example, recorded their deeds in Calaveras County, and those owing land in Aurora chose either a Nevada Territorial or a California location.

"The knife, the pistol, and Might is law at the present."
Visalia Weekly Delta, 4/13/61.

As the quote above states, the contest for the Esmeralda District was not settled before the most violent of events had been set in motion, events which began with the stealing of L. E. Wedertz's horse, stolen near Hoy's Station on the West Walker River between Antelope and Smith valleys in April of 1863, an event which brought about a chain of reactions which concluded with the following report from Aurora to Governor Nye by County Commissioner Samuel Youngs: "All quiet and orderly. Four men will be hung in half an hour." And so, on February 9, 1864, a powerful vigilante committee had ended a reign of violence which, because of the lack of one legal body, had seen the creation of a powerful, open, criminal force.[1]

Both the State of California and the Territory of Nevada elected officers from Aurora before the end of September of 1863. Dr. John W. Pugh was elected to the Nevada Territorial Council by the same electorate that sent Timothy Machin to the California Assembly. At the same time the California Legislature was busy granting toll and other franchises for the town of Aurora, and Nevada did the same. Meanwhile, Nevada and California had agreed to appoint a boundary commission, which acted with the United States Surveyor in determining the eastern boundary of California, the eastern boundary of Mono County; and the same line which became the western boundary of Nevada, the western boundary of Esmeralda County. As may be imagined from the

42

The bearded man standing inside the fence and to the right is pioneer George Albert Green. To his right is a daughter, Minnola Green. To her right, standing outside the fence and holding a dog is a son, Leslie Albert Green. This picture shows the old Green residence on the road from Carson to Aurora and Bodie. The fine old stone building still stands on the site of what came to be known as the Nine Mile Station and Ranch; the spot was a very busy stage stop during the boom days of Aurora and Bodie, and it was to this station that young Sam. Clemens came to visit, a visit that Clemens claimed helped his partner and himself lose their rich Auora claim. George arrived in California in 1849 with his father, Amos Green; in New Hampshire they had operated a family sawmill. After mining successfully near Marysville, the Greens acquired a sawmill, followed the rush across the Sierra to establish a sawmill at Green Creek at the base of the Sweetwater Mountains. This mill, hauled over the Sierra by ox team, was one of the first in Bridgeport area. Their main business was, however, supplying lumber to the towns of Aurora and Bodie. At the Nine Mile Ranch, the six children of George Green grew up, went to school, married, and moved away. George Albert Green died in 1915 and was buried at Bridgeport. Photo courtesy Lucille Eugenia Lewis Fallon.

43

above, there were many very interested parties. This Sage Brush Survey, as it came to be known, was a slow process; and it was not until September 16, 1863, that Aurora had been reached and shown to be in Nevada.

Prior to this discovery, strange events had occurred in Aurora. In June and July of 1863, Governor Nye appointed an entire set of county officials and ordered Chief Justice Turner to open court in Aurora. California had its own set of officials for Mono County, and Judge Baldwin held court as its representative. Double courts and double officers allowed litigants to choose either a California or a Nevada judge. Also, the term of office for Mono County officials elected in 1861 had expired, and an election was necessary. But instead of one election, two were held in Aurora in September of 1863, shortly before the boundary survey had reached the town. The polls for Mono were in the Police Station and those for Esmeralda in the Armory Hall; since both polling places were on the same street, many voted at both places. By the end of the month Aurora was shown to be three miles outside the California line, and many disappointed Californians claimed that a bend had been made in the surveyed line in order to exclude the rich Esmeralda District.

Among the unusual outcomes to the September election and the discovery that Aurora was in Nevada was that many elected officials refused to leave Aurora. William Feast, Mono County Treasurer, conducted business from Aurora until his death in 1864. The sheriffs elected by the two counties had agreed to name the other as deputy, whoever was elected. In this manner, Sheriff Frances of Esmeralda appointed Sheriff Teel of Mono as deputy, and neither left Aurora. Meanwhile, William Feast had helped R. M. Wilson transport the Mono County records from Aurora to Bodie and on to Bridgeport. In June of 1864 an election determined that the Mono County Seat would remain at Bridgeport, Owensville, located near Bishop, having lost in the contest. Thus was the history of the organization of "the first of the mining counties east of the Sierra Nevada."[2]

1. Thompson and West, *History of Nevada,* p. 423.
2. Coy, *California Boundaries,* p. 81.

Main Street, Bridgeport, looking southeast. To the viewer's left can be seen an old stone sidewalk laid between the Allen House and Bryant's store. To the right is the old Allen Stable. The larger building to the right is the shop. To the left of the stable is the granary building and the store of Dave Hays. At this time, the stable and buildings adjoining were owned by W. P. Brandon. Photo courtesy M. Bryant.

Old Bridgeport, circa 1879, showing its once distinctive New England atmosphere. This photo was taken from near the old Towle home and shows the Kirkwood residence at the extreme western end of Main Street. To the viewer's left is the Dave Hays & Bro. Store, the Allen House Stable, and the Leavitt House. On the right is Stanton Saloon, the Hughes Blacksmith Shop, the Loose Building, the Allen House, the Bryant Store, and the Jesse Summers home. The old Severance Blacksmith Shop can be seen to the right rear of the Stanton Saloon. Also on the right side of Main next to the Allen House was the home of J. N. and J. J. Dudleston, father and son; both were County officials. Note the absence of the Courthouse.

The County Seat

The election of June 14, 1864, between Owensville and Bridgeport, determined that Bridgeport would remain County Seat within the newly established boundaries of 1863. Since the County was already leasing a courthouse, a building located on the east side of the East Walker River and on the north side of the road, it was not long before the County Seat somewhat anchored itself by purchasing this building.

The American Hotel, the first Mono County Courthouse within the 1863 boundaries, located on the north side of Court Street. "Accommodations for County Officers are not in keeping with the general appearance of the town. The Court House, so called by courtesy, we presume, is an old tumble-down structure of very dirty boards, split up into dens designated as offices for Sheriff, Clerk, etc. The Court Room is in the second story." Bodie WEEKLY STANDARD, 9/9/78. Photo courtesy J. Brandon.

The building had been owned by W. M. Weaver who, in 1865, sold what was then known as Weaver's Hotel to J. C. Kingsley. The sale of the property, also known as the American Hotel, included the kitchen, bar, and bedroom furniture; the fixtures, perhaps, allowing for some necessary variety in frontier county business. In 1866 the County also leased the entire second floor of the Bryant and Reese store, located across the street from the American Hotel.

46

When the County purchased the American Hotel property from J. C. Kingsley, the building was already too small to handle County business and officials complained of closet-like offices. The rush to Bodie in 1877 created extremely pressing needs for governmental space, and in 1879 the Board of Supervisors received at Bridgeport a petition to order an election for the purpose of voting on the question of removal of the County Seat to Bodie, the most heavily populated Mono County community at that time. The Board, however, refused to acknowledge the authenticity of the signatures, and then it acted quickly to quiet any contest for County Seat by letting out bids for the construction of what is now the present Court House, completed in 1881.

The original courthouse, the American Hotel, was sold by Mono County at public auction in October of 1883 to A. J. Severe, who hauled it to his ranch where the building was used to store hay. "To what uses has this noble structure come at last", commented the local editors.[1] In October of 1887 the original Courthouse Lot was sold at auction, and in December of 1892 Washington P. Brandon moved his house across the river where it remains today near the site of the first Mono County Court House located at Bridgeport.

The Bridgeport Courthouse is a masterpiece of Victorian architecture that has dominated the town since its completion on April 1, 1881. The architect and superintendent of construction, John Reed Roberts, saw his plans actualize as his partners, Charles B. Anton and Samuel Hopkins, both of Bridgeport, carried out the construction. James B. Caine, a Massachusetts contractor and architect who had settled in Reno, was also involved in creating the design. Today, the Courthouse is one of the few remaining structures that reveals what was once the New England appearance of old Bridgeport. The following report, from the *Bridgeport Chronicle Union* of March 26, 1881, presents every detail of the construction:

> *This imposing Courthouse is in the main seventy-four by eighty feet, including wings. It being in the form of a Greek cross . . . The main foundation walls and partition footings are of large flat-bedded rocks, at a depth of two feet in the ground and three feet base, well grouted with liquid cement with 1¼ inch anchors built in the same ten feet apart, by which the main walls, sills, etc., are secured. The exterior masonry of the foundation*

1. *Bridgeport Chronicle Union*, 10/6/83.

to the height of thirty inches above ground, is composed of large blocks of cut granite (andesite), the work of Thomas Muckle & Brother of Bodie, and is strong and neatly executed. The main wall sills are 8 by 10 inches, with corner and center wall posts of similar size, all well-tenoned and pinned to sills and plates. The studding for same is 2 by 8 inches set 14 inches apart, diagonally boarded and bridged with similar material . . . studding, etc., is throughout diagonally boarded with 1 by 10 boards laid close-jointed, and 1¼ inch redwood rustic laid on same. The interior of main walls, partitions and ceilings are diagonally furred with 1 by 2 inch strips placed one foot from centers; lathed and three coats of plaster on same. The first and second story floor joists are 2 by 14 inches, set 14 inches apart, well-bridged and deafened between them. The floors are 1¼ inch Oregon pine, tongued and grooved. The roof is well-constructed in proportion to the wall . . . the cords are 8 by 10 inches, and the straining beams 8 by 12 inches and braced proportionate; ceiling joists, rafters, etc. . . . the gutters, valleys and conductors connected with the roof are of No. 24 galvanized iron, and are, with the roof, well-coated with metallic fire proof paint. The main walls are forty feet in height, from the front of which extends a magnificent cupola, twenty-five feet high, surmounted by a 25-foot iron flagstaff . . . at the main front entrance are two spacious vestibules, outer and inner, leading to hallways, ten feet wide, extending to the rear entrance. The side entrances are of a similar design, communicating with hallways of the same width, and connecting with the main hallway. From the main hallway, at right angles, is the staircase, ten feet wide, with a neat and massive newell post, buttress string balusters and handrail, made of Spanish cedar. The first and second stories are each sixteen feet in the clear in height. The first comprises eight spacious offices, two burglar fireproof vaults, storerooms and pumproom. The second is exclusively for Court purposes, comprising two Superior Rooms, each 32 by 40 feet; two Chambers, with closets; a room for attorneys, and two jury rooms, connecting with a hallway ten feet wide. The rooms are well-ventilated and have an excellent water supply from a tank, on the roof, of 3,000 gallons

This early photo of the Mono County Courthouse shows a large post leaning against the left front corner of the Courthouse. The purpose behind the post was brought to light when M. A. Bryant recalled that since the main road passed around the corner and on to Emigrant Street, there was a great deal of travel across the present Courthouse square. The post was put up to keep teamsters from running into the corner of the building. The house to the right may be the Donnel residence. About the time this photograph was taken, the Board of Supervisors came up with the following: "Information having been received that some of the Offices in the Courthouse are being used for sleeping purpose and the Board not deeming a safe practice of doing and that the same might affect the insurance in the building it is ordered that no office or department of the Courthouse shall be used for sleeping purposes nor shall any person or persons be allowd to sleep in said building except the janitor thereof." ROUGH MINUTE BOOK, BOARD OF SUPERVISORS, Oct. 3, 1881.

capacity, from which the fire hydrants, basins, etc., are supplied. The windows are exceedingly large and each is glazed with two French crystal sheet glass, supplied with inside white cedar blinds . . . The finish, all mill work, about $7,000, were done at the Verdi Planing Mill, at Verdi, Nevada . . . The brick work, plastering, cornices and center pieces are the work of McGee & Troy, of Reno . . . The painting and graining are by Smith and Crapp, of Bodie, who have sustained their well-earned reputation in that branch, the tinting, oak, ash, and walnut graining not being surpassed in the State . . . Of the $31,000, the County assumed $26,000, the balance falling upon the six bondsmen . . .

Starting at the left: J. D. Murphy, George Delury and unknown. Jail is to the right of the courthouse and shows fenced jail yard.

The Delury family moved from Bodie to Bridgeport in the 1890's. Delury served as Mono County Clerk.

Judge R. M. Briggs was installed in his new quarters and the Court immediately began its first business, that of the trial of Morton for stealing bullion from the Standard Con. Mining Company at Bodie. Residents formally christened the Courthouse by forming a torchlight procession, members of which bore a dog kennel on a bier as a representation of the former Courthouse. They met in the Courtrooms and exchanged speeches. Judge Briggs had been elected to the Superior Court in 1879, having been a lawyer and newspaper editor in Amador County, which he represented in the Assembly of 1858. The Illinois native had come to California in 1852; a long sufferer from "congestion of the lungs", Judge Briggs died at Bridgeport December 8, 1886, while serving his second term. O. F. Hakes was appointed Superior Court Judge of Department No. 1, as Briggs' replacement, and was elected to the office in 1888.

Presiding over Department No. 2 was Judge Marcus P. Wiggin, appointed by the Governor on April 16, 1880, in compliance with legislation which provided for an additional Mono County Judge. Wiggin, elected for a term of six years in the November election of 1880, inherited an unusual case that dated to the creation of Mono County and eventually formed some decisions that led to his removal from office.

The Mono County taxes for 1861-62 were collected in Aurora, those for 1863 were not. The treasury soon became exhausted and outstanding warrants remained unpaid. When the County Seat was settled at Bridgeport, the Mono County officials refused payment on all previously issued warrants on the ground that the expense was incurred in and for Aurora, and that Esmeralda County should pay them. "There are outstanding now some $20,000 of these old warrants, the larger portion of which have been collected together, and a suit is now pending to compel Mono County to pay them."[1]

The warrants had been collected and the suit had been filed against Mono County Treasurer Z. B. Tinkum by none other than Patrick R. Reddy, the notorious one-armed lawyer. The suit that Reddy prepared called for the Treasurer of Mono County to pay out of the General Fund, 51 warrants equaling $16,000 all of which Reddy was owner and holder. The warrants dated from 1862 to 1863 and were all drawn upon the County Treasurer of Mono County by R. M. Wilson, County Auditor, and all were endorsed: "Presented and not paid for want of funds, Wm. Feast, County Treasurer." Warrants later in date had been paid out. The defendant, Tinkum, denied the authority of Wilson and Feast, and denied their official existence, denied any County government of Mono County before 1864, and alleged that neither Feast nor Wilson were eligible to office at all, being non-residents of Mono County and non-residents of California. The principal issues were: was Aurora ever in the State of California, were there any legal County officers of Mono County between February 8, 1862, and December 13, 1863? After a great deal of research and examination, Judge Wiggin found that Reddy was not entitled to the relief sought. The case was of vital interest to taxpayers of Mono,

1. Thompson and West, *History of Nevada*, p. 403.

a suit for $24,000 more hung on the decision, the interest alone amounted to $50,400.

In February of 1883, the *Reno Evening Gazette* reported that Reno friends of Judge Marcus Wiggin would be surprised to hear of charges against him, the first charge appearing in the form of a protest filed by Mono County District Attorney W. O. Parker. The charge indicated that while acting as Judge of the Superior Court of Mono County Wiggin took a fee of $500 for attending to a case before the Board of Supervisors. The second charge noted that in a probate case before him, Wiggin ordered the Administrator to pay about $2,000 into Court; it was charged that Wiggin took possession of the money and postponed the hearing of the matter for about a year. The charges were enough to cause the California State Assembly and Senate to order that Marcus Wiggin be removed from office.

A Grand Jury in the Bridgeport Courthouse. From the viewer's left are Barney Patterson and Andrew Smith. In the back row against the wall are, from the viewer's left: Will. Cargill, Earl Hayes, Baxter Barnes, John M. Sawyer, Frank L. Wedertz, Chris or Fred Mattly, and Charles Stewart. In the lower row are Laffe Holmes, Dad Walters, Ed. Brandon, one armed Barney Peeler with spittoon, Bill Adair, Jack Sharkey, and Albert Brandon. Seated front center is Pat. R. Parker.

Settlers of Big Meadows

A few of the first prospectors and miners to enter Big Meadows recognized the agricultural and livestock potential of the valley. One such traveler who passed through the Big Meadows noted that it was the only spot on the trail from Sonora to the Mono Diggings where a meal and feed for cattle could be obtained. It was October of 1860 and the traveler had passed the Joseph Garretson Ranch, at what is now the Sario Ranch at Huntoon Valley, and had continued south along the trail until he soon entered the luxuriant meadows where Whitney & Co. operated an extensive ranch. At this time a man named Marsh also operated a ranch seven miles farther south, about where the Point Ranch now is. Most of the stock owned in Monoville was ranched at Marsh's. He lived in a sod hut on the east side of the valley and prospected at Dogtown Creek.

The first to have settled Big Meadows were William T. and brother G. A. Whitney, who arrived with a man named Green in 1859-60. They built a log house for Green on the east side of the valley and the brothers took up land on the west side. Their extensive holdings included what has come to be known as the Upper Day Ranch, the land between Buckeye Creek and the foothills. At this time land was taken up by possession, or preemption, the idea being to settle on land so as to establish purchasing priority and to seize the land before others could.

Under an Act of 1853, Congress donated to California 500,000 acres of School Land. The State issued warrants to settlers who wished to purchase them—the land was unsurveyed and there were no nearby land offices at which settlers could record claims. Such were the means by which settlers took up land in Big Meadows; possession was the rule. The situation brought about at least one serious conflict in which Sidney Huntoon shot a man who had jumped a portion of Huntoon's land; they were both lucky as the ball from Huntoon's gun struck the ribs and passed around just under the flesh of the victim.

In September of 1861, much of the land in Big Meadows was surveyed and mapped to protect the claims of the settlers. Aside from the Whitney brothers, those holding land at this time included E. H. Perry, A. D. Allen, Kelso, Rufus Hanson, G. C.

After the death of her second husband, Almond Huntoon, Elizabeth Anne Butler married Jesse McGath, who had arrived in Big Meadows in the early 1860's, as he is mentioned in Whitney letters of 1863. He owned ranchland on the West Walker, the old B. B. Bird ranch, and land in Big Meadows in 1863-64. In correspondence with W. T. Whitney, McGath mentioned that he had became wealthy but had lost it all in the decline of Bodie. He boasted that he could still ride a horse from Bridgeport to Carson City in a day. In 1898, McGath earned his income by driving the mail stage between Bodie and Bridgeport. The McGath home was at the present site of Slick's Court and was later moved to the rear of the present Bridgeport General Store. He died in 1917 aged 84. The old McGath residence at Bodie may still be seen; it is located on Green Street and was built in the summer of 1879. It was and still remains the handsomest residence in Bodie.

Hanson, W. J. Clements, Charles Snyder, Sidney Huntoon, B. F. Jones, A. Bronson, M. Durfee, F. Moullen, T. Magilton, Joseph Garretson, A. Bell, and George Ault.. C. R. Waterman, one of the earliest had already sold to Alex Bell and Solomon Townsend. Lamb and Smith, who owned 320 acres sold to John C. Nowlan; the property included a house and corral and was about twelve miles north of Monoville. G. W. Marsh sold his 320 acres to W. W. Williamson; the property was bordered by Wise's; such was the activity in 1861.

William T. Whitney returned to Iowa in 1862 and correspondence between William and G. A. Whitney provides a firsthand account of settling in Big Meadows. In addition to the two Whitney brothers, George Byron (By) Day and J. J. Coddingtor were part of the Whitney Company, both of the latter eventually separating and forming their own interests. The booming camp of Aurora, which was in full blast in 1862-63, served as the market for what was raised at Big Meadows. There, at Aurora, Whitney & Co. operated a hay yard and stable in connection with the Big Meadows property.

56

In November of 1862, Coddington had returned from a combination business trip and spree in San Francisco. By Day was busy hauling hay and lumber to Aurora, and Kelso was busy raising cattle. Business was good. In February of 1863 there was little snow on the ground and G. A. had bought slabs at the Buckeye Mill for $20 and By Day and another had hauled them to the ranch to fence the upper line. The use of slabs instead of wire was a common practice, and they were nailed horizontally to posts set in the ground. Activity at Aurora was now unbelievable. Coddington was making money fast and James Barnes had just sold fifty feet of mining ground for $800. One friend had made so much that he paid $2,100 for a diamond pin. Over fifty men a day were

A J. W. Towle photograph of Bridgeport Valley (Big Meadows) circa 1900.

Chas. Elliott of the pioneer Big Meadows ranching family. Charles taught school at Bridgeport for several months in 1870. It was a big family, four sons and four daughters. Photo courtesy Alice Dolan. This may be the same Charles T. Elliott who was later a United States Marshal.

entering Aurora, and Jesse McGath, Pike Richardson, Hodge, and Converse were all busy ranching at Big Meadows, Fales Hot Springs, and on the West Walker. In the spring, cattle and lumber brought cash on delivery. Hay was selling at $100 a ton, and Whitney would begin cutting in July. By mid-May Big Meadows was lively as pack trains had begun to cross via Sonora Pass. G. A. Whitney spent most of his time at Aurora marketing the ranch, which had been irrigated heavily so that there was more hay than ever before.

Suddenly life became all too exciting when Whitney found that his Aurora roommate had been accused of being too friendly with another's wife. The husband blamed them both so they packed six shooters and derringers until the roommate purchased the man's wife for $100. At the ranch, hay was being quickly cut and drawn in by Pike and pressed. Four tons were cut for their own oxen. In October of 1863 the hay was still not all in. The Whitney Co. sold timberland at this time to W. G. and Frank Heslip for $500 cash and $1,500 worth of lumber, which was delivered at the rate of two thousand feet per month from the pioneer lumbermen. A big ditch was cut for the Heslip sawmill and this extra water added to the ease of irrigating. The Whitney Co. now had three ox teams consisting of twenty-two yoke of cattle and three well equipped wagons. So far that year they had sold $7,000 worth of hay; the expenses had been about $3,000, not bad for 1863 in Big Meadows.

In March of 1864 both Whitney and William E. Elliott, a nearby rancher, remarked that it was very dry; water in the rivers

58

A gathering in the yard at the Elliott ranch. From the viewer's left are Leslie Elliott (holding parasol), Mrs. Brown, unknown woman, Mrs. Elliott, Mr. Elliott, Mrs. Palmeeter, Hattie Barnes, Joe Brown, Mamie Parker White, William O. Parker (seated and smoking a pipe at the extreme right.) Photo courtesy Alice Dolan.

was low and there was little snow in the mountains. Elliott complained that Robinson Creek was low because Z. B. Tinkum kept water back to use in sawing logs. Yaney, Leavitt, and Thomas and William Pickle were all mentioned. Aurora now showed signs of decline and money was scarce. A. J. Severe, for example, let a contract to build two miles of fence at 40 cents a rod.

In the fall of 1864 Aurora regained a little economic life, but hay prices were low. Whitney, in March of 1865, drove horses across to the San Joaquin Valley and noted that it was his first trip over the Sierra since the spring of 1860. G. A. Whitney was making plans to join his brother in Waterloo, Iowa.

George Byron Day, who had acquired half of an 800 acre parcel of Whitney land in 1865, took over, Whitney having left for Iowa. In 1868 Day acquired another 320 acres north of Elliott. The old Elliott ranch house stands near the curve in Highway 395 north of Bridgeport. Among those ranchers remaining in Big Meadows in 1868-69 were John Dawson, W. H. Bell, Sol Town-

59

Almond and Moses Huntoon, the latter wearing boots.

Napoleon Bonaparte Hunewill, pioneer rancher and lumberman. A native of Maine and one of the first to settle Big Meadows. A son, Frank E. Hunewill, was born at Woodside near San Francisco in 1860. From there the Hunewill family traveled by ox team across the Sierra to Carson Valley and on to the Aurora excitement. The founder of the present Circle H Ranch soon became the principal lumberman of the area as Bodie mines were discovered and building became a major industry. Photo courtesy Allice Dolan.

send, George W. Ault, J. A. Barnes, Nat. Luce, J. C. Murphey, N. B. Hunewill, D. O. Waltze, Steele & Stewart, Jack Severe, Sidney Huntoon, M. McCullough, Kelso, and Kingsley.

In July of 1868 the Sonora road remained closed by snow yet it was 104 degrees in the shade in Big Meadows. Three teams had made it over the Sierra to Leavitt Station but were unable to ford the raging West Walker River. In April of 1869 W. T. Elliott wrote that he had passed his best winter at Bridgeport since his first in 1863. It had been very mild. His stock, which was increasing, brought good prices.

The winter of 1874, was, however, very rough, and Elliott lost at least forty head of cattle. Many of them froze their feet so that their hoofs came off. The Elliotts, W. T. and his brothers Charles, and W. F. were old Mono residents. W. F. served as Superintendent of Schools in 1879. E. R. Elliott became a successful farmer in the San Joaquin. W. T. remained in Big Meadows, built the old ranch house mentioned above in May of 1882, and continued ranching into the 1900's. The property is now the Dressler Ranch.

Road Building

Bridgeport Valley was not easily penetrated. The Sierra wall forms the western side of the valley. The West and East Walker River canyons were long in becoming accessible roadways into the valley from the north. From the south, the Indian trail, and later the whites' wagon road, crossed Bridgeport Canyon, one of the few natural and wide passes, to connect with Mono Lake Basin. To the east, the valley is flanked by a range of rugged pine nut covered hills and mountains. The task of building roads and breaking trail in such country was rugged, the job of improving and maintaining the roads was never-ending.

Roads connecting Bridgeport with towns and mines often followed old Indian and white foot trails and were constructed under

The winter of 1860 saw Dave Hays building a small cabin on the Sonora Mono Road at Eureka Valley. The cabin grew to this imposing stage station, the walls of the lower floor being made of hand squared logs. James J. Welch, a close friend of Dave's had a cabin at Niagra. Strawberry was conducted by Major Lane, and J. W. Brightman established Brightman's Flat. H. L. Leavitt was at Leavitt Meadows. and Sam Fales completed the stage stops for this line with his Fales Hot Springs. At this time, about 1860, they were known as snowshoe men and carried the mail between Sonora and Bridgeport. Photo courtesy the Tuolumne County Museum and Alice Dolan.

State franchises, developed by companies who generally sold stock in order to pay for construction costs, and the owners were allowed to collect toll. The roads were later bought by the County, most roads being purchased after 1890 and into the 1900's, a time during which the roads had become devalued property. Most of the toll road franchises were valuable only as long as the mining com-

61

Mrs. Sam Fales (Diana Muir). Photo courtesy Alice Dolan.

munities they connected continued to produce ore. Once the mines failed, a road costing thousands of dollars to construct could often be purchased for less than one hundred dollars. The road franchises in and about Aurora were especially unusual since both California and Nevada Territory granted franchises in the same area until the fall survey of 1863 showed Aurora to be in Nevada.

One of the most important roads for this area was the Sonora and Mono Wagon Road which connected the rich Esmeralda and Bodie Districts with the produce of the San Joaquin and the industrial products of San Francisco. It was first planned during the Aurora excitement of 1860-63 but was not completed in the sense of being fairly passable to larger wagons until after the Aurora decline in the mid 1860's. The road followed the old Indian and emigrant routes across Sonora Pass, but it followed, more closely than the latter routes, the course of the Stanislaus River. The road began about thirty miles east of Sonora at Strawberry Flat, where a stage station was developed, and wound its way along the ridges on the south side of the Stanislaus River until it reached the Kennedy Meadows area where it crossed over the river and followed a small tributary to the crest of the Sierra. From the crest, the road dropped sharply along the eastern scarp of the Sierra to Leavitt Meadows, where H. L. Leavitt operated a station. From there the road traveled over meadows and low ridges to the present junction at Highway 395 near Fales Hot Springs, where Sam Fales operated his Station. At the junction itself, A. Mack and family built a Station often called The Junction House. Mack

Teamster Reason Barnes. He is listed in the MONO COUNTY GREAT REGISTER OF 1882 as a native of Ohio aged 53.

This photo by Frasher shows the venerable pioneer Sam Fales standing before the boiling Fales Hot Springs. Sam was a story-teller of wide reputation, and his hot baths and mud baths were popular treats and remedies. Fales was an early arrival in Big Meadows, locating land in various places in the early 1860's until he settled at the hot springs and built a stage station. Minnie, a daughter of Sam's, married Clay Hampton in 1886; over 150 people attended the wedding at Fales Hot Springs, and the Bridgeport Brass Band was there. She later married J. G. Pimentel, a Mason Valley sheep rancher. One winter in the 1890's, Sam and his wife snowshoed in to Bridgeport. The trip of 14 miles took two days; the first night was spent at Huntoon Station. Both Samuel and his brother, Thomas, were natives of Michigan.

was an early settler, had owned a saloon at Monoville in 1861, and was once County Clerk. When he died in 1881, and his wife in 1884, the Rickey family took over the station. Mrs. Mack was the daughter of Henry Rickey. One of her sons, Maurice, later became a senator. At the height of travel over the Sonora and Mono Wagon roads during the summer boom years of Aurora and Bodie, the amount of travel was staggering. Foot travel, pack trains, and wagons of all shapes and sizes crossed over and back before fall storms closed the pass and forced them to travel the longer route via Placerville.

The State had appropriated bonds for the Sonora and Mono Wagon Road construction, but the cost was well into the hundreds of thousands of dollars. Contracts were awarded to individuals who were then responsible for constructing a specified portion of the road. Before the actual construction began in 1861, the route was passable to foot traffic and pack trains; desperate emigrants had already dragged wagons over the granite walls, sometimes totally dismantling them, sometimes inching them up and down with block and tackle. Stock was driven over but often had to wait, in the early spring, until the swollen West Walker River at Leavitt Meadows allowed them to ford. The route was gradually widened and improved, but the high elevation has, from the very beginning, allowed the road to be nothing more than a seasonal route, the first heavy fall storm traditionally closing the route, the first teams and wagons to break through in the spring traditionally opening it. Many foot travelers who tried an early crossing suffered the effects of becoming snow blind and frostbitten.

> *Mrs. Blasdell and Mrs. Hilton arrived from Sonora yesterday and left for their Bishop home this morning. They had a fatiguing trip over the Sonora road on account of the depth of snow, having to assist in breaking the road. The snow is ten feet deep in places, and the ladies had to wade through the snow waist deep, and had to camp out, and suffered much from the cold. They had an experience they do not care to duplicate. 10/30/97 Bridgeport Chronicle Union.*

In coming from Aurora to Bridgeport in the early 1860's the traveler went two miles down Esmeralda Gulch, then three miles southwesterly up Bodie Creek, then three miles to the head of Rough Creek and across Table Mountain. It was here that Dave Hays froze several toes, held up in a cave, and decided to build

The Sulphur Springs Station at the time it was occupied by the Wiley family. A popular stage stop, as it was located on the road from Wellington to Aurora and Bridgeport.

a better route to Aurora down the East Walker Canyon. From Table Mountain the road went east three miles to the head of Long Canyon (Aurora Canyon) and down its mouth eight miles and west one mile to the bank of the East Walker River at Bridgeport. The promoters and owners of this toll road were I. Garrison, J. M. Garrison, A. J. Severe, J. N. Dudleston, G. Raymond, J. B. Hawkins, D. H. Haskell, M. Bixby, and Jacob George.

As mining camps spread, the County experienced a growing network of toll roads connecting Aurora, Bodie, Bridgeport, Lundy, Mammoth, and the Dunderberg. In 1870 both the West Walker and East Walker Canyons were formally invaded by the organization of toll road companies who quickly finished work that was begun in the late 1860's. The West Walker River Toll Road Company was organized by B. G. Hartshorn and Richard G. Watkins. It traversed the west side of the canyon walls and ran from Antelope Valley to the Junction Station below Fales Hot Springs. On the same date, April 4, 1870, The East Walker and Munckton Road Company was organized by A. F. Bryant, Dave Hays, and J. J. Welch. This was a more favorable route to Aurora than the Table Mountain route, and the latter was gradually abandoned except for some summer travel. The toll house of the East Walker Company was just south of the present highway bridge at the cliffs. There Henry Hays manned the station into the 1900's.

65

Henry Hays, toll collector at the East Walker River toll house. Collection of Alice Dolan.

Fales Station-grey bearded man 6th from right is Sam Fales. — J. W. Toles, photo.

In 1869 a road was run from Big Meadows, from near the present Point Ranch, to Castle Peak (Dunderberg) by O. Kimball, H. Marden, and D. O. Waltze. Since the Dunderberg mines were not too profitable, the toll road was not a successful business venture. Bodie, on the other hand, brought such a huge volume of travel for several years, that the Big Meadows and Bodie Toll Road was a very valuable property. J. C. Murphey was president of this corporation, and his stage station at Clearwater, located a mile or two up the Bodie Road from the present Highway 395 junction, was a heavily patronized stop. In December of 1878, for example, a traveler noted that he met forty lumber teams all pulled by from four to twenty animals. Receipts over the road for a slower winter month were $1,862.34, far more profitable a location than many mines. The rates of this road were typical:

Buggy teams	$1.50	Horseman	.25
Loaded wagon & two		Pack animals, each	.25
animals	1.00	Hogs & sheep, each	.05
Each additional pair		Loose stock, each	.05
of animals	.50		

By the early 1880's the County began to exercise some control and required that holders of toll road franchises present a quarterly report of expenses and receipts. Mono County road building gained a little fame when D. M. Geiger built Geiger Grade to make a more direct east-west connection between Bridgeport and Bodie via Aurora Canyon. Geiger, who had built the famous Geiger Grade at Virginia City did not repeat his success here; the road was too steep. The motivation for building it is clear when one notes that revenues over the Virginia City Geiger Grade were estimated to have been over $1,500 per month for a ten year period. He moved on and settled in Inyo County in 1886.

Travelers on Highway 395 who climb Sherwin Grade may be interested to know that in 1892 J. C. Sherwin sold his road, the Round Valley and Mono Mills Toll Road, to Mono County for $125. This was the usual price and the usual fate of toll roads as the County gradually developed its road system. In 1896, toll roads remaining within the County were the Bodie and State Line, 7-10 miles; the Big Meadows and Bodie, 15-40 miles; the East Walker River, 13-20 miles; the Mono Lake and Lake District; and the Sonora and Mono, 17-70 miles. During the height of the toll road franchise business not all travelers were cooperative. T. N. Machin, while writing of Monoville and Aurora noted that

Joseph W. Kingsley, a native of Massachusetts, early settler of Big Meadows. His father, J. C. Kingsley was known as the old man at the Bridge. J. W. later went into the livery stable business at Bodie. Photo courtesy Alice Dolan.

he became so frustrated at having to pay a toll for every few miles he traveled that he drew a gun on one toll keeper and had him point out the road for several miles. A Mono Lake rancher, on the other hand, found that each trip to the post office cost him a toll payment. He complained to postal authorities and succeeded in having a post office established at his ranch.

The Yosemite-Tioga Pass road was completed to the rich mines of the Great Sierra Con. at Bennettville, just west of Tioga Lake, in 1883. It was just a little over 56 miles in length, was built by white and Chinese labor in 130 days of blasting and hand excavating at a cost of over $1,000 per mile. The work was awesome and brutal. By 1888 the road had fallen into such disuse after the collapse of the Great Sierra organization that W. C. N. Swift purchased the franchise for $10. It was not until 1909 that the road was extended in passable condition down the east side via the treacherous walls of Lee Vining Canyon. One of the most stimulating of experiences in the early 1900's was an auto trip up Lee Vining Canyon; the one way road and the 2,000 foot drop to the canyon floor was real adventure.[1]

1. Trexler, *The Tioga Road.*

Kingsley, Parrish and Patterson

Most of the story of old Bridgeport is best revealed through the stories of the pioneers themselves, and one of the first families to arrive in the valley was the Parrish family, which arrived in 1865 when it became the County Courthouse, and in September Bryant's, probably under the present Bridgeport Reservoir, but their barn and house was located on the south side of Main Street. Charles Parrish, born in 1864, claimed to have been the first child born in the valley, and in 1866 the marriage of E. A. Parrish to J. W. Kingsley united two pioneer families.

The Parrish house was just east of Kingsley's house and 160 acre ranch that bordered the south side of Main Street in the vicinity of the present Dept. of Motor Vehicles office. Kingsley arrived with his father, J. C. Kingsley who was known as the old man by the bridge. J. C. Kingsley owned the American Hotel property in 1865 when it became the county courthouse, and in September of 1865 he sold his interest in his farming and dairy property to his son. The property consisted of the dwelling house, on the south side of Main street, 18 milch cows, and twelve beef cattle; hogs, chickens, and cheese were included as was the right to the brand. Joseph W. Kingsley also acquired the 160 acre Parrish ranch and buildings in town. The old Parrish house became the property of Judge G. E. Goodall, who lived in it and had his law office there.

J. W. Kingsley, a native of Massachusetts, was a New Englander, like many early settlers of Bridgeport. He went on to Bodie where he opened the City Livery and Feed Stables, which he purchased in July of 1879. Kingsley Street in Bridgeport bears the old family name.

In 1899 James H. Patterson died at Bridgeport; he had arrived in the the late 1850's with the rush to Monoville. He and a brother, R. S. Patterson, operated a sawmill near Monoville, engaged in mining, and built a sawmill near Bridgeport in Patterson Canyon in 1870. J. H. Patterson was born in Ohio and had six brothers and sisters. Two sisters were Bridgeport residents, Mrs. G. B. Day and Mrs. Mary Barnes; R. S. Patterson was killed while

The old Bridge Crossing showing a team of mules pulling three coupled lumber wagons. The two wheelers are horses. In the rear can be seen the store of L. E. Wedertz and the J. W. Towle house, the present Huggan's residence. Photo circa 1880. Courtesy M. A. Bryant.

holding the office of Sheriff. James turned to mining and discovered the first mines of the Paterson District high on the slope of Mt. Patterson in the Sweetwater Mountains, both the district and the mountain being named in his honor.

70

"Completed—The new bridge over the river at the foot of Main Street is completed, and on Thursday morning C. M. Stewart's big 14-horse team, with four wagons, was the first to cross it. It is 51 feet long and 16 feet wide, and is the most substantial one in the County, and has probably been built for less money than any of its size, the labor and getting out stone for the abutments having cost but $450, the County having furnished the lumber, timber, and iron-work, the cost of which will be seen when the Supervisors meet to pay the bills. On the way in from Carson, Stewart had one of his best horses die on the road." 11/13/97, BRIDGEPORT CHRONICLE-UNION.

The Bridge,
the Crossing,
Main Street

The footbridge connecting Bridge and Court streets across the East Walker River marks the site of the old crossing, the first wagon bridge, and what was previously the main highway route until the course of Highway 395 was changed to its present route, west of the old Towle house. .

It was around this old crossing, or ford, that Bridgeport evolved as a settlement. Here teamsters crossed, rested, and watered their animals and then moved on east, across Sonora; south, to the Mono and Benton areas; west, to Bodie and Aurora; or north, to the supply centers of Carson and Reno. The high banks along the river on either side of the lower fording area were favorite camping spots for local teamsters and loggers. Lewis Ladd recalled that a favorite stopping spot was the high bank north of Court Street where Brandon later moved his house. It was there that the old Courthouse was located after the election of 1863.

71

A J. W. Towle photo showing sheep fording the river at the crossing just north of the present footbridge and old wagon bridge. The area around Brandon's Barn was nice meadow land irrigated by water from Bryant's ditch. The slab fence was characteristic of enclosures. The property shown across the river is on the north side of Court Street.

On the south side of Court Street, near the present Sturgeon residence, Bryant, with helpful advice from his friend, H. Marden, located a store. Marden noted that it was an almost daily occurrence to find at night from fifty to seventy-five head of oxen turned out to graze, and the teamsters campfires dotted the riverbanks. Severance had arrived from Calaveras County and added to the settlement at the bridge by erecting a blacksmith shop. An 1863 correspondent referred to old man Kingsley, a butcher shop, two blacksmiths, and many old wagons about what he called the settlement at the Bridge.

By October, 1863, in response to the Aurora excitement, needs for feed, meat, and lumber at the mining camp, quite a settlement had grown east of the old crossing. Expectations were high that the Sonora-Mono Wagon Road would soon be finished to add volume to the trading taking place at the Bridge. In March, 1864, the same correspondent referred to the settlement as Bridgeport, the bridge and the many New Englanders combining to create the naming. Soon Big Meadows was known as Bridgeport Valley. Growth was slow, however, Bridgeport having polled only 142 votes in the September election of 1863.

The old log and rock-cribbed bridge, surrounded by the low fords on both sides at which livestock crossed, and the more recent truss bridge, serve as examples of the evolution of the site, the latter bridge accommodating early auto traffic.

A J. W. Towle photo of Bridgeport circa 1900, taken from on top the Coasting Hill. The old course of Main Street can be plainly seen as it enters town from the viewer's lower right, and leaves town by making a right angle at the old Courthouse and a second right angle west.

73

THE STANTON BUILDING

The accompanying photograph, taken by J. W. Towle about 1901, shows a team of 14 animals on Bridge Street in front of ground on which the Walker River Lodge now stands. The three coupled hay wagons, complete with man astride the wheeler, are probably headed for Bodie. The first building behind the wagon is the old Stanton Saloon, one of the first buildings in Bridgeport. In the early 1860's the saloon was operated by James N. Booth, who probably built it during the Aurora boom. At that time it housed a billiard table in addition to its bar fixtures. J. D. Dawson bought the property in 1868 and sold it to William Henry Stanton in 1873.

Stanton, a native of New Hampshire, was a farmer until saloon-keeping took over. An 1879 inventory showed the following necessities of saloonkeeping: nine pictures, one mirror, one small glass, ten lamps, one alcohol lamp, three card tables, fourteen bar room chairs, one set of scales, one billiard table, twelve cues, one set of ivory billiard balls, seventeen tumblers, five beer glasses, seventeen cocktail glasses, nine poney glasses, two decanters, one lime squeezer, two lime knives, seven flower vases, two candle sticks, pool boards, cribbage boards, six spittoons, three Colt pistols.

Stanton died in September of 1890, aged 44, having suffered from tuberculosis for ten years. Next behind the Stanton building can be seen the gallows frame, used in shoeing oxen, and shop of blacksmith P. G. Hughes. Beyond the gallows frame is the Allen House.

Main Street, Bridgeport looking west. The Kirkwood home can be seen at the end of the street. J. W. Towle photo.

Snow appears in the shadow of the front of Dave Hays Store. Beyond the Allen House, the Bump Market, and Bryant's Store can be seen a cluster of smaller buildings. From east to west these buildings housed the following: The Crowell Building, used as a millinery shop by Mrs. Crowell and later as a post office; it is the dark building with the shed roof. Next was the Crowell residence. Mr. Crowell had originally built the shed roofed building as a store for Mrs. A. C. McKinnon who was in operation in 1883. Next was Brown's Store; Sparks' Barber shop, formerly Judge Virden's law office; the fire station, and Kirkwood's Saloon. The buildings changed hands and tenants rapidly, several saloons being housed there. J. W. Towle photo.

MAIN STREET: NORTH SIDE

The photograph of Main Street looking west shows, to the viewer's right, the Allen House, the rear portion of the hotel housing the kitchen. Beyond the Allen House is the Bump Market, the Bryant Store (note railed upper porch), and four or five buildings which include the postoffice, several saloons, the fire house, and Brown's Store. The large building whose roof stands below and to the left of the Court House cupola is the old Simmons Saloon at the present site of the Trails Restaurant. At the left side of the photo is the front of the store of D. Hays & Bro., and the Allen House Grainery and Livery Stable.

Main street was the scene of a variety of activities, and in the spring, summer, and fall months it was crowded with freight, lumber, and produce wagons en route to Bodie and Aurora. Hay wagons were a common sight and loose cattle, horses, and sheep were also driven through the street by the hundreds. On one occasion a single band of 1,300 sheep was herded through town. An occasional bull fight was a common sight, and spectators seated in saloon chairs made wagers from the raised boardwalks in front of the bars. But, in comparison to Lundy and Bodie, Bridgeport was quiet. On one occasion, in 1888, the local editor complained of too much yelling and shooting, but his following report was the usual scene:

Dull is no name for the times in this town and county at this time. There is absolutely nothing going on out of which a fellow can manufacture an item. The dogs won't even fight, and our horses are too well bred to run away and injure a body, or mash a buggy; and our community is too moral and religious to get up any fights or domestic unpleasantness that would be public property— and so items are as scarce as hen's teeth. The town is quiet as a cemetery, the practicing of the band now and then, being all the noise one hears excepting when school lets out." BRIDGEPORT CHRONICLE-UNION Feb. 10, 1894.

One of the highlights of the 1890's on Main street, was a footrace, which took place in August of 1895. Ed Brandon of

Bridgeport and Cecil Burkham of Bodie were the contestants. It brought to town a large number of Bodieites and others, and the hundred yard course was marked out from the foot of Main Street uphill to the Rickey House. The starter fired his pistol and the two dashed off, but Brandon slipped and Burkham won for Bodie.

In the spring, when snow run off flooded Main Street, the intersection of Main and Sinclair Streets was opened on the north of Main by a temporary bridge put up between the Simmons Saloon and the saloon across Sinclair to the east. A ditch ran across the street near this point and passed just to the west of the Simmons Building, but it could not accommodate the water. In 1889 a ditch was constructed through Kirkwood Avenue and across to Emigrant Street. This relieved the situation at the Sinclair intersection. Another ditch crossed Main Street to the north just below the old Stanton Saloon and emptied into the marsh now covered by the Walker River Lodge. Water is especially close to the surface in the Big Meadows during the spring. The early ranchers spread it over the valley through ditches from Summers, Green, and Dogtown creeks at the southern end, and Robinson, Buckeye, and Swauger, which enter from the east and north. The paving of the Main Street in 1906, and the construction of the reservoir and raised highways has interfered with the flow of run-off across the meadows.

One of the curiosities of old Bridgeport was Professor Hatfield's Tonsorial Parlor, a small shop built there in 1880. Bridgeport boasted of having a barber who had been the second one in business on the Pacific Coast. Hatfield was in the Mexican War and landed at San Francisco on February 9, 1849. He bought a lot on the corner of Kearney and Washington streets for $200 and opened a barber shop in a tent. He sold it for $300 and finally drifted to Bridgeport. He followed the gold camps to Clinton and then drifted on.

Bridgeport's tonsorial needs were met by Joseph Sparks, who operated a small shop in a little brown house on Main Street. The shop was the former office of Judge Virden and was west of Joe Brown's Store.

Mrs. McKinnon's Millinery Shop was also located on that portion of Main Street, and in 1889 Mrs. Crowell took over the business.

The present home of Wesley Berreyessa was the home of Judge Goodall, Doc Sinclair, and J. M. Sawyer. The Leavitt House

The old log and stone cribbed bridge is shown here spanning the East Walker and supporting three coupled lumber wagons. In the foreground is a ford for livestock. In the rear is the Brandon Barn. The site is the present footbridge.

and the Hopkins home completed the block. Across Sinclair Street from the Hopkins house was a large barn that was probably used in connection with the Leavitt House as Leavitt sold it, in 1886, to C. C. Turner and W. P. Brandon. It had large sliding doors in front and later became the property of A. D. Waltze, who operated it into the 1900's.

In old Bridgeport, Main Street was a dead end at the Kirkwood home, at the north end. Instead, the main route north turned right at the Courthouse and followed School Street to Emigrant, at which point wagons turned left and followed the present lane past the Day Ranch and on in a straight line to the corner of the old Elliott ranch house. The iron fence around the Courthouse was a late addition, having been erected after 1900, and it was common practice for teamsters to cut their rigs across the Courthouse square; in fact, some collided with the corner of the building. To protect further collisions, a cedar post was attached to that corner of the building at an angle and anchored in the ground.

Travel over the roads was rough and one never knew what to expect; wrecks and runaways were common and mail delivery was a rugged business. Mail arrived by rail at Hawthorne, Nevada, from which point it was carried by stage to Bodie and then on to Bridgeport. Many times during the winter season the mail stage was forced to return to Bodie after having traveled only a mile or two. Sometimes the mail was carried to Bridgeport by a man on snowshoes, and often a man from Bodie and one from Bridgeport met halfway. Then each fought his way back through heavy drifts and blinding snow.

79

The Mono County Chapter of the California Pioneer Society was organized in 1879 with 38 members. Members had to be 49er's in order to join. This photo was taken on Admission Day 1884 at the Courthouse. R. M. Folger is holding the large book. To his right, Henry Hays. Behind Henry to his right stands H. L. Leavitt. White-shirted C. M. Stewart stands front center. The last two men in the second row at the viewer's right are Pike Richardson and Sam Fales. Others here are A. F. Bryant and Dave Hays. In 1897 the following members were left: W. Witherill of Benton, R. Christin of Bodie, A. F. Hector of Bodie, A. F. Bryant, R. M. Folger, Dave Hays, F. M. Pike Richardson, William Boardman of Coleville, Andrew Thompson of Mono Lake, and Joseph Hunt of Coleville. Like that of R. M. Folger, their stories of trips to California were all filled with adventure.

Tbe FolgeR BRotbeRs

Much of the adventure of the California gold fields was in the danger of getting there, as the narrative of Robert Macy Folger, the pioneer journalist of Bridgeport, reveals. Folger was born in New York in 1820, was later a member of the Society of Friends, and at eighteen became head bookkeeper in a large broker's office. Soon he opened an office for himself, and then, on January 11, 1849, he left New York on the schooner *Anthem,* bound for Sacramento. Folger and nine other members of the thirteen cabin passengers had formed the Winfield Scott Mining Company. Captain of the schooner, Thomas Eldridge, of Mystic, Connecticut, was familiar with the route through the Straits of Magellan as he had made several sealing voyages into the Pacific in the 1830's.

The *Anthem,* a center-board schooner of 200 tons, had been built expressly for the California trade and was a fast sailer; on the fourth day out of New York she passed the point where the steamer *Panama* had broken down five days from New York. She also passed the *Josephine,* which had a nine day start on her. The *Panama* returned to New York, and it was arranged that she would tow the *Anthem* through the dangerous straits, Captain Eldridge piloting the steamer. But before the two ships were able to rendevezous, the *Anthem* encountered a heavy gale which lasted three days, and as she was blown over the treacherous Laurel Shoal a sea wall followed her. Captain Eldridge thought that she would founder, but the sea sunk and the *Anthem* rode over the shoal. Although the schooner was hove to with a hawser and spar off the bow, she drifted 120 miles east in 72 hours.

During the last day of the storm, on March 6th, they came upon the *Sarah Parker,* which was returning to Nantucket from a whaling voyage of three years. The captain was looking out for whales on his return home, having not heard of the discovery of gold in California, and when he sighted the *Anthem,* with her deck crowded with red-shirted men, he suspected that the schooner must be a pirate ship and ordered the *Sarah Parker* to crowd sail. The chase lasted for three hours until the *Anthem* closed and hailed the *Sarah Parker.* Both ships hove to, and the second mate of the *Anthem* recognized the captain of the whaler, with whom he had

81

formerly sailed on a whaling voyage. The excited crew of the whaler then boarded the *Anthem* and begged their captain to let them stay and go on to California, but their captain offered to promise to forget whaling and to make sail for Nantucket to fit out for California. In due time the *Sarah Parker* anchored in San Francisco Bay.

The *Anthem* went on and anchored at the Northern Passage for the *Panama,* but the latter passed by and missed sighting the schooner, assumed that she had been lost in a storm, and sailed on. The arrival of the *Anthem* at San Francisco, on June 28, 1849, marked the arrival of the first schooner; and it was notable that the insurance companies had refused to insure her, a center-board, to make such a trip.

The *Anthem* sailed on to Sacramento, arriving there on the first of July. The next day she returned to San Francisco and was back in Sacramento three days later with a full cargo and 200 passengers at thirty dollars per head. The *Anthem* belonged to Colton Hoxie & Co., of Sacramento. In September she made her last trip and was sold for use in the Galveston, Texas line. During the three months service on the Sacramento, her owners realized a fortune from her earnings.

Folger stepped off the *Anthem* at San Francisco near the center of what is now the financial district, the corner of Washington and Montgomery Streets. The Winfield Mining Company soon dissolved, and Folger went on to purchase several lots in Sacramento where he went into the hardware and machinery business. He imported the first quartz mill that was erected in Nevada County, at Gold Flat, near Grass Valley, which ruined its owners. He sold, to Moffit & Co., the boiler punch which punched out their $50 octagon slugs. He served as chief of the Sacramento Fire Department, but in the big Sacramento fire of November 2, 1852, he lost it all. From the wreck he drifted into journalism with his brother, Charles, who had arrived in 1851. Alex and Frank, also brothers, soon arrived.

But previous to R. M. Folger's journalistic ventures, he made a trip back to New York, via Panama, leaving January 1, 1850, on the steamer *Oregon.* With Folger traveled General Fremont and several influential politicians who were en route to Washington to urge statehood for California. Captain Norton and Bayard Taylor were also passengers. The *Oregon* was built for the Pacific Coast prior to the discovery of gold, and her cabin was limited

Alexander Coffin Folger of the pioneer journalistic team of Robert M. and A. C. Folger. Photo courtesy Alice Dolan.

to thirty passengers. The sale of tickets commenced at an early hour and continued until midnight, when over 450 steerage passengers were booked— the rate was $150 to Panama, and only one ticket was sold to an applicant. The time to and from Panama was restricted to not less than 21 days, so sail went up and steam went down when the wind was favorable. The *Oregon* stopped at Monterey, Santa Barbara, Mazatlan, and Acapulco.

The steamer arrived at Acapulco late in the evening, and most of the passengers spent the night ashore, well armed, for the inhabitants were hostile. The next morning, Captain Pearson went ashore to dine with the Commandant of the Port, but when the two returned the Captain was knocked down and beaten by Captain Norton and soldiers were ordered to charge. The Americans retreated to the steamer. Fremont called for volunteers to retaliate, but Captain Pearson had recovered and detained them. The nearly disastrous episode had grown out of an old quarrel between Norton and Pearson, but the rest of the trip went smoothly. Folger returned and, in 1852, brought his wife to Sacramento.

Robert and Frank Folger started the Sacramento *News* in 1861; it lasted two years and the former moved to Ione, Amador County, and started the *Ione Chronicle*. The paper was moved during the Alpine mining excitement, first to Markleville and then to Silver Mountain. There, with his brother Alex, R. M. Folger published the *Alpine Chronicle* until the fall of 1878 when they moved to Bodie. At Bodie Robert and Alex published the

Mono-Alpine Chronicle, then changed it to the *Bodie Chronicle,* which lasted two years. In 1880, while still publishing the *Bodie Chronicle,* the brothers started the *Bridgeport Union.* The first number of the Bridgeport paper appeared on May 15, 1880, and with the completion of the new Courthouse they were assured of plenty of County printing, so they moved their Bodie plant to Bridgeport, merged the two papers, and created the *Bridgeport Chronicle-Union.* Their office was on the northeast corner of Bryant and School Streets.

Their only competition was *The Mono County Relief,* an offshoot of the *Bodie Miner,* which began in 1886 and lasted about a year. The other County papers were mining sheets, and a great deal of banter, ridicule, and sarcasm was exchanged through the papers as the various editors saw fortunes rise and fall. Being an agricultural journal in the midst of mining camps, the *Union* was dubbed "the Onion", and the quiet County Seat was referred to as the Mormon Camp, with Uncle Bob Folger as Chief. In contrast to other County papers, the *Chronicle-Union* was very serious in tone, and the brothers were known for their patriotism and stout defense of ethical journalism. The American Flag was kept flying at their office, and it was reported that they had been responsible for the idea of having the Flag flown in every schoolhouse. Aside from their membership in the Society of Friends, the brothers were very active in practically each social event and organization in Bridgeport. At the time of his death in July of 1899, Robert M. Folger was the oldest journalist on the Coast. Alexander Coffin Folger carried on the work of reporting, composing, and printing the paper, and with his death ended a continuous run of forty years of journalism. They had known and been associates of many pioneer journalists: John I. Ginn, Orlando Jones, Fred Elliott, Hiram Childs, J. J. Curry, J. E. Baker, Fernando Frost, Wells Drury, Myron Angel, Lying Jim Townsend, Harry Fonticella, and many others of Comstock and California papers. Then, on April 23, 1906, appeared Vol. 1, No. 1, of the *Bridgeport Chronicle-Union,* published by Montrose & Montrose, pioneers of Bodie and Lundy.

Perhaps one of the greatest compliments was paid to the senior Folger by Orlando Jones of the *Bodie Miner,* with whom he had often verbally dueled: "When Uncle Bob Folger sharpens up that pen of caustic which he wields he makes a fellow's flesh quiver."[1]

1. *Weekly Standard News,* 4/27/81.

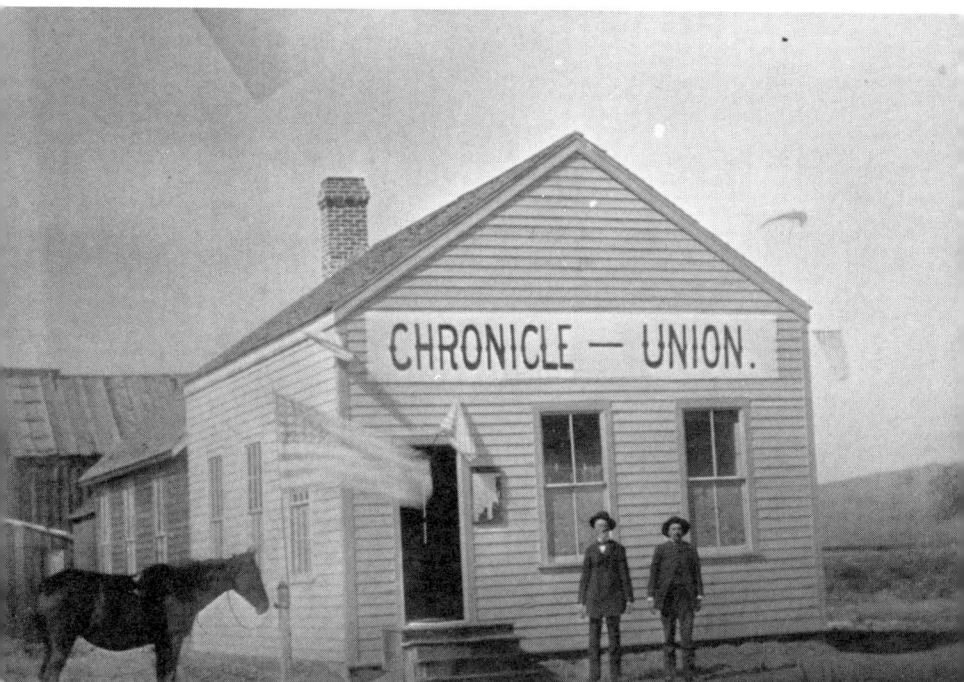

The patriotic office of the BRIDGEPORT CHRONICLE-UNION newspaper office and residence located behind the present courthouse at the site of Annex No. 1. Standing in front is grey bearded Alex Folger. The horse used in deliveries stands patiently.

Hotels

A native of Northern Ireland, Andrew Harper Allen, and wife Olive, settled in Bridgeport Valley in 1863; he was to build one of the finest structures in old Bridgeport, the Allen House, located on the north side on Main Street. The land on which the Allen House Hotel was built was originally owned by Bryant and Reese, who sold the land to H. C. Ladd. There Ladd built a small structure known, in 1864, as the Bridgeport House.

Lewis Ladd recalled that soon after his father arrived in Big Meadows in the fall of 1862, after a six-week trip from Los Angeles by ox team, his father built the first house in what is now the townsite. The land was covered with sagebrush which the settlers grubbed out. In 1865 Ladd sold to Allen, and the old Bridgeport House became a part of the Allen House when Allen eventually expanded the business. The Ladd family eventually settled on Emigrant Street in a house that had been moved over from Bodie.

85

The genial Andrew Harper Allen, builder of one of Bridgeport's finest hotels, the Allen House.

The Allen House, built in 1877 by Peter Nye and Dave Gilchrist, was an imposing Victorian structure that housed many travelers en route to or returning from the mining camps. Across the street, at the present site of the Office of the Department of Motor Vehicles, was the Allen House Livery Stable and Barn, operated in connection with the hotel. Allen also owned a 160 acre ranch bounded on the north by Kingsley.

Upon his death in 1894, "Andy" Allen left a son, Arthur Allen, and three married daughters: Mrs. James Anton, Mrs. E. A. Murphey, and Mrs. L. A. Murphey. In 1895, the Allen House be-

One of Bridgeport's finest structures, the Allen House, which burned to the ground about 1914. At this time Rickey was the proprietor. The squared stone foundation and the ornamental corners were identical to those of the Courthouse. The stone sidewalk can be seen to the left, running to Bryant's Store. Among the celebrities are A. F. Bryant in grey suit, Billy Rickey third from right, one of the Browns on the first step with beard, dark suit and hands in pockets; to his left and leaning against the right post is Will Butler.

came the property of Mrs. W. H. Rickey, of Rickey's Station as the old station at the junction of the Sonora and Antelope roads was then known. The hotel then became The Rickey House until September of 1897 when it was sold to W. P. Brandon, the sign being changed to the Brandon House. One of the curiosities of the property, aside from the complete bar and kitchen in the hotel itself, was a granary built opposite the hotel by W. Rickey in 1895. It stood on cedar posts two feet above the ground. The posts were capped with inverted milk pans so as to make the building mouse proof. The old granary is now all that is left of the old Allen House and stands behind the present Brandon residence where it is used as an out-building. Old timers recalled that in 1886 "Andy" Allen could be seen riding in a fine buggy from

Mr. and Mrs. Hiram L. Leavitt, proprietors of the Leavitt House, and granddaughter May Waltze. Photo courtesy Alice Dolan.

the carriage works of his brothers, W. A. Allen & Co., of Akron, Ohio. A fire, thought to be deliberately set, destroyed the old Allen House about 1914.

The old Leavitt House, now the Bridgeport Hotel, has been a popular retreat since its construction in 1877. Hiram L. Leavitt hired Sam Hopkins to build and supervise the construction; the result: the Leavitt House and the marriage of Miss Ida Leavitt to Samuel Hopkins.

Leavitt sailed from Boston, arriving in San Francisco in February of 1853. After spending some time in Sonora he returned to the East and brought out his wife and daughter. They lived at Sonora until about 1865 when they crossed the Sierra and settled at what is now known as Leavitt Meadows on the West Walker river. Prior to his settlement, the area was called Indian Valley. The Leavitt family, which now included two additional children, Charles and Alfred, kept a stage station and engaged in ranching at Leavitt Meadows until he completed the hotel and moved into Bridgeport, abandoning a favorite stage stop on the old Sonora-Mono road. His business, however, moved with him to the new townsite of Bridgeport and the heavily traveled route to Bodie found many registering at the Leavitt House.

Leavitt served as County Judge of Mono under the old California Constitution. He was a native of New Hampshire and died in 1901, aged 77. Charles M. Stewart purchased the old hotel, and his daughters Maude and Emma Grace have preserved and enhanced the fine Victorian atmosphere of Bridgeport's oldest hotel.

A convoy of old trucks parked in front of the Leavitt House. Beyond the Leavitt House can be seen the front of the Sam. Hopkins home and the large Leavitt Stables, operated by Waltze.

George Hughes, son of Patrick.

Patrick G. Hughes, hammer and horseshoe in his hands, stands at the door of his blacksmith shop. The geared machine to the viewer's left was used to bend strap iron in making and repairing wagon rims. To the right is a horse drawn scraper leaning against the front wall. Photo by J. W. Towle circa 1885.

Blacksmithing

Immediately west of the old Stanton building on the north side of Main Street was the Hughes' Blacksmith Shop, the accompanying photo showing Patrick G. Hughes in the doorway of his shop. Tradition, and a good deal of recorded history, holds that on this spot stood the first building in Bridgeport, the blacksmith shop of T. B. Severance. In the early 1860's the shop was jointly owned by Severance, H. C. Ladd, and Moses Robinson. The latter sold his interest in 1865 to Hughes for $100, and in 1867 Hughes acquired sole ownership. Hughes, in 1871, purchased a competing shop located across the street, closed it, and remained a Bridgeport resident for many years. In addition to the shop, Hughes owned a ranch of 160 acres, and the family occupied the now weathered two-story residence on the south side of Main Street just west of the present Brandon residence. Two sons, George and William, assisted their father in the shop until the advent of the automobile brought an end to the blacksmith trade. Patrick had used the heavy gallows frame outside his shop for shoeing oxen; the laborious task included raising the animal off the ground and tying back and anchoring the rear legs.

Other old Bridgeport blacksmiths were A. Kirkpatrick, T. M. Glover, Randolph, and John A. Campbell, the Hughes shop surviving them all.

The P. G. Hughes home. Photo courtesy J. Brandon.

91

Norman and Annette Huntoon.

Huntoon Station, west side of Highway 395.

The Huntoons
and
Huntoon Station

In 1883 the Booker Flat Hotel at Bodie, owned by Almond Huntoon, was moved to Huntoon Valley, about ten miles north of Bridgeport on Highway 395, where Almond and his wife, Elizabeth Anne Butler, operated a new business, Huntoon Station, a stop for weary travelers and teamsters. The building was located near the site of the present brick Sario residence; across the street was a saloon.

In September of 1890, Almond, then 56, who had been ill for many years, committed suicide. He had arrived from Canada in the early days, with his brothers, had done well, but lost it all in the collapse of Bodie. Seated in the chair in the photo of Huntoon Station is Annette Huntoon. The girl standing is May Huntoon Walters. In 1895 Annette Huntoon operated a store at the old station. In time the building was sold to Peter Latapai and torn down.

The Huntoon brothers included Lansing, who ran a saloon in Bridgeport in the 1880's, John, Norman, Moses, Sidney, Frank, and Philander. In 1864, Sidney bought a large amount of land in Big Meadows; in 1868 he owned 640 acres; and among his possessions were four yoke of oxen and three mustangs. The ranch land was located in the northeast portion of the valley. In 1882, he sold 800 acres to James Sinnamon, the transaction including interests in the McCullough, Obenchain, and Severe ditches. In 1884 Sidney sold his ranch to John C. Murphey; and, with his wife, returned to Canada. Kirman and Rickey eventually acquired much of the old Huntoon ranch, thus adding to their growing cattle empire.

The Huntoon Building stood on the northeast corner of Main and Sinclair. Lansing, as noted, ran a saloon there; in 1885 C. B. Anton reopened the property while, across the street, Almond Huntoon reopened the old Loose corner. The editor noted that "this gives us only five licensed saloons in town. Scarcely enough, but we must try to get along with these few, considering the times are rather tight."[1]

1. *Bridgeport Chronicle-Union,* 12/24/87.

Sheep shearers at Huntoon Station and ranch.

May Huntoon and husband Frank Walters lived in the old Huntoon home, the present Bettancourt residence. The large family of brothers had many interests: dairying at Huntoon Valley and Bodie, ranching at Big Meadows and in Nevada, saloonkeeping. Huntoon Valley, Huntoon Creek, and Huntoon Valley in Nevada remain as reminders of this pioneer family.

In March of 1883 in a Bridgeport saloon, J. W. Powell and John Huntoon were scuffling when Huntoon kicked at Powell and hit a pistol in his pocket. The pistol struck the floor, discharged, and the ball hit Huntoon in the right knee. His leg was amputated. John was a man of stalwart physique and continued to be active. Several months later, he suffered a painful injury when a horse he was riding fell on the stump of his leg; he carried on and, in 1885, was reported to be building a saloon at Clinton. He died in 1898 at the age of 55, having resided in Bridgeport over 20 years. John can be seen seated in front of the saloon at Huntoon Station, in the accompanying photograph, at the right of Edward Wedertz, the latter standing near the door and wearing a white coat. The taller man to the left of Wedertz is Moses Huntoon. The photograph was taken by Towle in 1896 as the *Chronicle* reported that, in May, Wedertz, Day, and Duke were shearing their respective bands of sheep at Huntoon's ranch.

Second from left, Bertha Wedertz in front of home on Emigrant Street, Bridgeport.

Judge Virden Home—Judge seated, wife standing on his left.

James Logan

In February of 1892 woodcutter James Logan had delivered fifty cords of wood for County use. His wood lot was behind the *Chronicle-Union* office, from where wood could be quickly transfered for use at the Courthouse. Logan, a native of Canada, had married Bertha Wedertz. The photograph shows them at their home on Emigrant Street. From left are Jennie Box Mercer, Mrs. Bertha Logan, Mrs. Louis Ladd (The Ladd house was next door), James Logan, Alice Ladd. Logan held interests in the Masonic mines, having been a part owner of the Red Cloud Mine and having invested heavily in the Pittsburg Liberty. Fortune never came his way, and old-timers recall how Logan, armed only with axe and lunch bag, walked through town each day to cut pine nut wood in the hills east of town.

Ed Wedertz House.

The Virdens, Jefferys and Wedertz

David Jefferys, at one time Mono County Clerk. He resided in what became known as the Virden home and was a native of Great Britain. During the flush days of Bodie, he was Clerk of the Big Meadows and Bodie Toll Road. Photo courtesy Alice Dolan.

In March of 1895 Judge W. H. Virden was busy fixing up the old Jeffreys residence opposite the Courthouse, at the present site of the Sportsmen's Inn Restaurant. Judge Virden, seated in the illustration with his wife standing at his side, was elected Superior Court Judge in 1890.

> *"Large Crane — Yesterday morning Edward Wedertz shot a crane which had been hovering over town for several days. It stood four feet high and measured five and a half feet from tip to tip."*[1]

In May of 1887, Edward settled on more rewarding game and married Flora Sinclair, daughter of Bridgeport's "Doc" Sinclair. She is standing, in the photograph showing their residence on Kingsley Street, to the left of her husband and against the screen door. This had been the old Sinclair home. At Edward's right is his daughter, Carrie Rowena Wedertz. Edward was among the first to enter the sheep raising business in Mono, having formed a partnership with his father-in-law. He continued in sheep raising in Smith Valley, Nevada, where he served as County Commissioner of Lyon County.

99

The interior of the Court House Corner Saloon. Photo courtesy J. Brandon.

Court House Corner Saloon

The accompanying photographs show the Billiard Parlor, bearing the name of James Logan as proprietor, and the interior of the same building, which was known as the Court House Corner Saloon when the building was moved from Bodie to Bridgeport in 1883 by A. Seiler. The bar opened in May of that year; the absence of bar stools may be noted, as they were a later invention. Instead, customers stood at the bar or sat in chairs like those seen in the front of the building. R. Witford, J. M. Sawyer, and others operated saloons there at the site of the present Ken's Sporting Goods Store, the old building having been remodeled. Dave Le Roy, in black tie, stands at the rear arched doorway, the sign in Spanish, above his left shoulder, being for the enlightenment of enthusistic sheepherders.

101

George Bump

George Bump at his meat market, which he built next to Bryant's Store in 1895. To the left is the fence around the Bryant garden, and the bedroom off the store can be seen. To the right rear is the home of Louisa Brandon. At this time, the Bumps were living in the old Donnel residence near the Courthouse. In 1896 George, having discovered the pleasures of Twin Lakes, launched his new fourteen-foot boat, *The Mud Hen*: "It is a creditable piece of naval architecture and will carry a heavy armament, when its owner is in it."[1]

1. *Bridgeport Chronicle-Union*, 5/16/96.

Dave Hays, senior member of D. Hays & Bro., pioneer Bridgeport merchant. The Hays store was probably opened about 1870. He was established in Bridgeport in 1869 as one of the Elliott brothers wrote that Dave Hays was there.

The store of David Hays and brother Henry on south side of Main. Standing near the door is the proprietor, Dave Hays, complete with cap. To his right is Ella Cody Cain and Mrs. Hays. Seated to Hays' left is Alice Walker Hays; two children, Grove and Earl are standing. To the viewer's right is David W. Hays. Photo courtesy J. Brandon.

103

The home of Ben Miller; built by A. J. Severe.

Hays and Hayes

Four brothers, David, Henry, Maurice, and John, settled in old Bridgeport. Dave and Henry spelled their surname without the letter "e"; no explanation for the change has survived. Maurice Pease Hayes, who served as Mono County Sheriff, was the father-in-law of A. W. Brandon and was born in Bridgeport, Connecticut in 1843. Previous to his 1880 arrival in Bridgeport he had been a deep sea diver on the East Coast and had many stories which he related in Bridgeport, in the midst of the Sierra.

David was probably the first of the brothers to arrive in old Mono, coming to Bridgeport in 1869 where he entered the merchandise business with brother Henry under the name of D. Hays & Bro. David, born in Fairfield, Connecticut, in 1831, had arrived in San Francisco in 1849 on the bark *Trenton* after a voyage of six months. He recalled hunting game near San Francisco and in the San Joaquin Valley before reaching the gold fields of the Feather River. He then settled for a time in Tuolumne County and later conducted a toll station at Eureka Flat on the Sonora-Mono wagon road. In an 1867 trip across the Sierra to Aurora, he froze his feet and had several toes amputated. Once established in Bridgeport, David was active in road building, having taken part in financing and constructing roads to Clinton, Bodie, and the Dunderberg Mine. One property, the East Walker River Toll Road Company, was incorporated in 1870 by J. J. Welch, A. F. Bryant, and Dave Hays. Henry operated the station, built to serve the hoped-for needs of Munckton (a short lived mining camp at Dunderberg), into the 1900's.

The store and connected living quarters of D. Hays & Bro. was just east of the present Department of Motor Vehicles station, and the property included the brick warehouse, which remains at the corner of Main and Hays Streets, built in the 1890's. In December of 1895, carpenter Sam Hopkins built the wooden annex

105

Top row, from viewer's left: Ella Donnel Williams, Louisa Wedertz Brandon, Addie Donnel Kirkwood, and Clara Donnel Murphey. Bottom row: Washington P. Brandon, Judge John Murphey, Eugene Williams. Children: Melvin Murphey, Arnot Murphey.

on the warehouse so that the building could be used as a hall for the Odd Fellows and other societies.

The Edmistons, old Bridgeport residents, were related to the Hays through David's wife. J. J. Welch was a close friend as was J. W. Dennison, who died in 1889. He too was a native of Connecticut and arrived in California in 1852. He had been deputy assessor under Dave Hays in Tuolumne County and was afterwards elected assessor. He resided in Bridgeport twenty years and died as the result of burns suffered when he fell into a campfire at Twin Lakes.

The Murpheys

Standing at the left in the photograph is a member of the first graduating class of the University of California, Judge John D. Murphey; seated at the extreme left is Clara Donnel Murphey. Standing, from John's left, are Lou and Ed Murphey, all three being sons of John Carpenter Murphey, who left Ohio April 2 and crossed the Plains with a pack train to arrive in California on August 12, 1849. John came to Bridgeport in 1864; he was a lawyer and once served as District Judge and District Attorney of Mono County.

The old Murphey ranch of 160 acres was north of Bridge Street and included a house, lot, and stable. At the same time, in

The Murpheys arranged for photographer J. W. Towle along the east side of the fine old victorian home of Jesse Summers. Standing at the viewer's left is Judge John D. Murphey; seated below him is Clara Donnel Murphey. Standing to the left are two other sons of John Carpenter Murphey, Lou and Ed. Wives, mothers-in-laws and animals included.

1868, he also owned the 160 acre Moorman Ranch and operated Clearwater Station on the road to Bodie. A daughter, Ada, married Harvey Boone in 1889. Boone was a direct descendant of Daniel Boone and operated a number of 16-animal freight teams, a large hardware store in Bodie, and an extensive ranch in Bridgeport Valley, Boone Creek bearing the pioneer's name.

Another daughter married B. L. Simmons, who operated a saloon on the northeast corner of Main and Sinclair Streets. Judge John D. Murphey also served as Mono County Clerk and can be seen in many old photographs of county personnel.

The Murpheys on a camping excursion near Bridgeport.

The Murphey Boys from a J. W. Towle glass negative.

The Murpheys

Hunewill and Ladd

Washington P. Brandon

Washington P. Brandon, Bridgeport rancher and teamster, soon gained a wide reputation for his expert handling of large teams of horses and mules. It was his team, for example, that hauled the huge mining equipment up the treacherous sides of Lundy Canyon to the May Lundy Mine. The family came west from Iowa and first settled in El Dorado County. It was a large family, but the parents and several children died of arsenic poisoning. Washington moved to Mono County, acquired ranch land north of Court Street; the old house that he moved there still stands. Wash, as he was generally known, married Dorothea Wedertz and, later, Louisa Wedertz. Children, grandchildren, and relatives still reside in Bridgeport and Antelope valleys. Wash's sister, Helen, married Judge J. G. McClinton, pioneer editor, lawyer, and mining engineer of Aurora and Bodie. The Hayes and Brandons also became related through marriage.

The present home of J. Brandon, photo circa 1900. The woman at the door may be one of the Murphey family.

111

E. P. Butler, RENO, NEVADA.

A Rough Trip.—Wash. P. Brandon returned from Lundy about 3 o'clock Wednesday afternoon from his trip to Lundy with the machinery for the Lakeview mine.—He was four days getting the machinery up the hill to the works, one piece of his load weighing 15,185 pounds. Seventy men were employed to shovel out the road, the snow at that point being very deep, and his sixteen horses had no picnic on the trip. On his return on Wednesday night he was caught in the heavy snowstorm that raged that evening on the summit this side of Goat Ranch and had to camp without unhitching his team, and without hay to feed them. Teaming in the mountains in the Winter is no funny business.

The Stewarts

Mr. and Mrs. John W. Stewart.

In 1883 Mrs. J. W. Stewart bought the home pictured here from Frank Hessel in Bodie and had it moved to Main Street where it stood at the site of the present Redwood Court. It had cost Hessel $3,000 to have the house built during the Bodie boom; Mrs. Stewart purchased it for $175.

"Boone Home" corner of Kirkwood & Main Street, Bridgeport.

The Stewart ranch house now under the waters of Bridgeport Lake just west of the Harmon residence. Charles M. Stewart on porch. Photo courtesy Grace Crocker.

Charles McLeod Stewart and wife Emma Wedertz, married at Bridgeport by Judge Poe on Feb. 3, 1874. Emma was born at San Francisco in 1854. The couple had three children. Maude, who married Antone Berreyesa and had two children, Wesley and Emma Grace, the latter being the present proprietress of the Bridgeport Hotel. Maude later married Sam Cohen. A son of Charles and Emma was John Wesley Stewart who later did well in business at Tonopah and was a member of the Nevada State Senate. The third child, Grace, married Pat. R. Parker, son of William O. Parker and Judge of the Superior Court.

114

A sixteen-horse team leaving the old Stewart Ranch. The site is under the present Bridgeport Reservoir. The three coupled wagons are loaded with wool. Mt. Jackson provides the skyline. Photo courtesy M. A. Bryant.

Children of Charles and Emma Stewart: Maude, John Wesley, and Emma Grace.

Wesley Stewart, at the steering wheel, in front of the Stewart residence on Emigrant Street. Charles Stewart is on the hood. Patrick R. Parker is at the rear of the car wearing a pointed hat; Emma Wedertz Stewart is below Pat. Parker; Bertha Logan is stepping down from the car. Photo courtesy Grace Crocker.

John W. Stewart was one of several brothers who came to Mono County in the 1860's from New Brunswick. He married Ada Murphey, who, after John's death in 1883, married Harvey Boone. J. W. Stewart served as Assessor of Mono County in the 1870's and held ranching interests with his brothers, James Edgar, who arrived in Mono in 1872; teamster and rancher Charles McLeod Stewart, who married Emma Wedertz in 1874; M. Y. Stewart, who operated a hotel in Bodie. Mrs. S. A. Kirkwood was a sister.

The brothers probably came West in 1857 since another brother, William Stewart, a lawyer and Wisconsin State Senator, noted in an 1887 visit to Bridgeport that he had not seen his brothers for 30 years.

John Stewart, in addition to ranching, speculated in many areas. He hydraulic mined at Monoville just before his death. In 1880 he transferred to N. B. Hunewill and Wm. Irwin two sawmills, timber land in Buckeye Canyon, 1320 acres of timber land in By Day Canyon, a lot on the corner of Wood and Green Streets in Bodie, and all equipment formerly of Mayberry and Hill. The price was $10,000, a fortune in those days.

The large ranch that the family operated was located under the present Bridgeport Reservoir. There they had corrals, a house, and a barn. They also acquired the old Moorman Ranch, Charles M. Stewart operating it in the 1880's. Charles later bought the old Leavitt House, Wes Berreyesa, Grace Crocker, and Mrs. Edward Denton, being descendants of the Stewarts.

116

Charles M. Stewart on horseback at the upper Stewart ranch, also known as the Boone ranch. All of this is now under the waters of Bridgeport Reservoir. Photo courtesy Grace Crocker.

The Stewart generations: rear row from viewer's left, unknown, Grace Stewart Parker, Dora Wedertz Brandon, Emma Wedertz Stewart, Mrs. Ladd, Maude Stewart Berreyesa, John Wesley Stewart, Bertha Wedertz Logan. Front row from left: Grace Berreyesa Crocker, Antone Berreyesa holding Grace, Charles Stewart holding Wesley Berreyesa, and Pat. R. Parker. The photo having been taken at the Stewart residence on Emigrant Street.

Antone Berreyesa was the first graduate of Stanford University and a descendent of the Berreyesa family that came to California with the De Anza Expedition of 1776, arriving in what is now San Francisco. The family owned the New Almenden quicksilver mines, and three lost their lives defending its title. Bodie was his first teaching assignment. Antone knew boxing so Bodie did not cause him to take a fast stage out. He also taught at Lundy before coming to Bridgeport. J. W. Stewart's daughter married Antone, thus uniting two pioneer families.

This wagon was used to ferry people to Buckeye Hot Springs.

The elegant bath houses at Buckeye Hot Springs. Photo courtesy M. A. Bryant.

Buckeye Hot Springs

In 1884, Buckeye Hot Springs, located on a high bank above Buckeye Creek, in the canyon, was the property of A. J. Severe and J. C. McTarnahan. There they erected a bath house. In the summer of 1885 it was reported that the springs had become a popular resort for camping, bathing, and fishing. Elisha Gurney drove an express wagon out and back daily, the distance being about seven miles and west across the meadows. Severe had constructed the road, and a better building was being moved over from Bodie.

In the 1890's, C. E. Heath acquired the property by possessory claim and put in a 14 x 24 foot bath house. The following summer, Heath and his wife added a dancing pavillion. It became a popular spot for socializing, and a health spa for those suffering from aches, pains, and disease. The hot water was flumed across the ravine through which Buckeye Creek runs. Cold water was flumed in from the creek so that the bathers could mix it to a desired temperature.

118

William O. Parker, pioneer Bridgeport attorney.

William O. Parker

Born in Glasgow, Scotland, in 1842, William Owens Parker came to Oregon while still a young man and enlisted in Co. E of the 6th Oregon Infantry during the Civil War. Parker arrived in California about 1870, locating at Bridgeport about 1877 where he began a law practice.

Of the four children from his marriage to Annie Boucher Hine, only two survived. One was Patrick Reddy Parker, who was named in honor of Parker's close friend and fellow attorney, the notorious one-armed Patrick Reddy. P. R. Parker, who was admitted to the bar at age twenty-one, joined his father in practicing law at Bridgeport and became Judge of The Superior Court of Mono County.

The father, W. O. Parker was himself no stranger to Mono County Superior Courts. He had been removed from his office as District Attorney in 1882 by the then Superior Court Judge R. M. Briggs for "willful neglect of his official duties."[1] The action was brought against both Parker and his Bodie Deputy District Attorney, R. L. Peterson, for allegedly accepting $100 to stop prosecution of what was even then a totally unmanageable and restrictive Sunday Law. As Parker himself undoubtedly pondered, how could anyone seriously enforce a Sunday law in a town like Bodie? It was with great pride that he saw his son later assume the Superior Court Judgeship. Patrick Reddy Parker married Grace Stewart, uniting two pioneer families.

1. *Weekly Standard News*, 3/15/82.

More
Lawyers

John Merrick Sawyer and his three children. Standing at the rear is Nellie, who later married A. S. Bryant. To Sawyer's right is Robert, who later became a mining engineer and assayer and worked at Bodie and later Nevada camps. Lyna May Sawyer later married Frank L. Wedertz. The two girls were born in Bodie, Nellie in 1879, and Lyna May in 1881. Robert was born at Hawthorne, Nevada, in 1883. Sawyer's wife was Helen Anne Kernohan, daughter of Bodie's first resident family, Robert and Elizabeth Anne Kernohan. Sawyer was born in Ohio in 1848, served during the Civil War in the Sixth Iowa Volunteer Cavalry which was engaged in the Souix Indian troubles. John M. came West after the war with his brother, but they became separated and each thought the other dead. It was not until 1908, 37 years later, that John visited Souix City, Iowa, noted a Sawyer in the directory and discovered his brother. John M. died in 1926 at Bridgeport. He had at Bodie been in the dairying and hotel business; in Bridgeport in the 1880's and 1890's he was one of the more popular saloonkeepers. His residence was the present Berreyesa home.

George Whitman, attracted to the new County Seat, moved to Bridgeport from Aurora in 1863; he established his home and office in the old store of Bryant and Reese on the south side of Court Street. Whitman had sailed from New York on the ship *Panama* and arrived in San Francisco on August 20, 1849. In 1859 he was elected to the Assembly from San Bernardino County, and also held public offices in Los Angeles and San Jose. In Mono County he served two terms as District Attorney and was a justice of the peace. Whitman was a large man, at least 6' 4"; he died at his home in Bridgeport in 1885 at the age of 70.

The death of another pioneer lawyer, Judge J. E. Goodall, occurred in 1901. He had been Mono County Judge in 1864-65 and was a member of the Assembly in the Session of 1866. Goodall also served on the Board of Supervisors in 1878-79, at which time he was instrumental in defeating the attempt to have the County Seat moved to Bodie. In 1880 he was Registrar of the U.S. Land Office at Bodie. Like Whitman, he too was a justice of the peace. His residence was the old home now the residence of Wes Berreyesa.

120

To the right rear of the courthouse can be seen the jail and connected living quarters for the Sheriff of Mono County. The board fence around the jail yard was definitely substantial being ten feet high and made of tongue and groove boards one inch thick; girts and posts provided support, and waterproof paint was applied. The fence was built in 1883 by A. J. Severe.

Sheriffs, Jails and Badmen

Aurora, the first County Seat of Mono County, was one of the most lawless camps of the West, rife with Civil War unrest and supporting a large criminal element. A factor allowing for this situation was that both California and Nevada claimed Aurora and its rich Esmeralda District gold mines; the result was chaos in all areas of governmental jurisdiction, that of law enforcement being most confusing. But before the Boundary Survey of 1863 could be completed to quell the chaos and define the location of Aurora, a citizen was brutally murdered and his body set on fire. Outraged citizens immediately formed a protective committee, rounded up the most notorious criminals in camp, and, on February 9, 1863, executed Three-fingered Jack and three others on a hastily erected scaffold.

The first sheriff of Mono County, N. F. Scott, elected June 1, 1861, was killed during the Owens Valley Indian War of 1862 and G. W. Bailey was appointed to fill the office.[1] Confusion continued when, in the September election of 1863 (held at Aurora before the boundary survey was completed, which would show Aurora to be in Nevada), the candidate for sheriff to Esmeralda County, Francis; and the Mono County candidate, H. J. Teel, agreed before the election that both wanted to remain in Aurora whatever the election outcome. Both candidates won their respective offices, so Sheriff Francis appointed Teel to serve as

1. Thompson and West, *History of Nevada.*

121

Mono County Sheriff James Showers and wife. The former Comstock miner, and Bodie Mine foreman was appointed in 1880. He later moved to Los Gatos, and when he helped capture a horsethief there a party was held in his honor.

Deputy Sheriff of Esmeralda County. This left Mono County without a sheriff when Aurora was shown to be in Nevada. Seth Sneden filled the vacancy and became the first Sheriff of Mono County within the 1863 boundary, Sneden holding office until 1867 at the new Mono County Seat of Bridgeport.

The next excitement took place about twenty miles from Bridgeport at the booming camp of Bodie, between 1877 and 1882, when the Bad Man From Bodie emerged as a journalistic jibe at all bad shots, back shooters, cowards, drunks, and beaters of women. R. S. Patterson, Pete Taylor, James Showers and their deputies were kept busy during this period as the mining excitement rose and the population of Bodie neared 8,000, a sharp contrast to the pastoral Bridgeport and its 200 inhabitants.

As in Aurora, lawlessness at Bodie culminated in a vigilante action, the January 1881 execution of De Roche, who was taken, by the mob, from the branch jail on King Street and marched to the scene of his crime, on Green Street, where he had assassinated a Cornish miner who had objected to the Frenchman's attention toward his wife. Between 1879 and 1881 seventeen violent deaths had occurred in Bodie; 1,200 jurymen had been assembled, and these cases (all of which the County lost) had cost the taxpayers about $50,000.

The first and only legal infliction of the death penalty in Mono County was the hanging of Chow Yew at Bridgeport on December 12, 1878. Chow Yew had murdered another Chinaman at Benton; Yew was so weak from fright that he had to be assisted to the gallows by Sheriff Taylor and his deputy. As usual in California history, the Chinese was the scapegoat for the fears and crimes of the whites.

Out of the violent mining camps of Aurora and Bodie emerged a series of Mono County peace officers who resided at quarters provided for them at Bridgeport. Their jurisdiction included the mining camps of Benton, Bodie, Lundy, and Mammoth. Seth Sneden, Z. B. Tinkum, R. S. Patterson,[1] James Showers, Pete Taylor, C. F. McKinney, Watkin Morgan, and M. J. Cody were the sheriffs of old Mono County, whose adventures pose a rather strange chronicle of law and order. Most had been miners; most respected the individual but were often quite direct in methods, as Draper and Morton found out.

Draper and Morton, inmates in the Bridgeport jail, were heard making suspicious noises and were discovered making a key. Failing to elicit the whereabouts of the tools, the deputy trussed Draper by the thumbs, standing tiptoe, in which position Draper eventually disclosed the whereabouts of a small awl and a hand-saw concealed in a crack in the floor. Two months later, in April of 1881, the old wooden jail at Bodie was towed to the Courthouse Block at Bridgeport, and the following month brought the erection of a substantial board fence, 50 x 75 x 10 feet high, forming a yard around the jail. All these efforts seemed to only encourage an unusual tenant yet to come.

The Chinese were not all as submissive as Chow Yew, so Sheriff McKinney discovered after he had locked Ye Park in the Bridgeport jail for the murder of another Chinese. At 5:30 on the morning of December 16, 1882, the startled prisoners sounded the fire alarm in the old wooden jail, and Henry Donnel, the first citizen to respond, split open the jail door with an axe. Ye Park had escaped through a hole that he had burned in the floor; soon the fire destroyed all but the two iron cages. The loss was set at $2,000. Luckily there was no wind, and the flames had not spread to the Courthouse.

In February of 1883 Sheriff McKinney returned Ye Park, who had been captured at Carson City, to a temporary jail which

1. Patterson died of consumption in Oakland, *Esmeralda Herald,* 8/31/78.

Sheriff C. F. McKinney in Bodie Knights Templar regalia. "It took C. F. McKinney two days to get from Bridgeport to Lundy. Two horses gave out and he was forced to snowshoe in from Mill Creek." 4/1/83 DAILY FREE PRESS.

had been built to house the iron cells. The wiley Chinese had tried to elude capture by attempting to burn off a mole on his cheek; he also wore a false que. He now faced the additional charge of arson. In April, Sheriff McKinney took Ye Park to San Quentin, and the Chinese gave his word to McKinney that he had no intention of burning down San Quentin. Meanwhile, County officials hurriedly planned a new jail, a stone one which still stands behind the Bridgeport Courthouse. A well was drilled in the jail yard for additional fire protection.

The Grand Jury, however, did not relieve the embarrassed McKinney of any guilt in the Ye Park escape; and they reported that the Sheriff and the jailer had been very lax, yet no criminal intent was evident, although the Grand Jury very graphically noted "carelessness, stupidity, and negligence in the performance of their plain duties". It was discovered that prisoners had been allowed to freely roam outside; some worked for nearby residents and were paid for it. They were not even locked in their cells at night, and opium smoking was carried on late into the night. At least one prisoner had access to the office and to the drawer where the keys were kept. A key to the cell of a prisoner was taken on the day before the fire and was found in the possession of one of the prisoners. The Grand Jury further censured McKinney and future incumbents were warned.

C. F. McKinney, who was elected in 1882 and served two terms as sheriff, seemed to attract the unusual. Several months after the Ye Park affair, and the publication of the Grand Jury Report in the *Bridgeport Chronice-Union,* he had a prisoner in jail who had been arrested in Bodie for fighting. The prisoner did not want to eat in jail so Sheriff McKinney took him to a restaurant for breakfast. On the way they compared their Civil War notes, and McKinney mentioned that he had been captured by a squad of Morgan's men, who were ragged and desperate, and told to take off his clothes and boots, the latter article being especially scarce among the Confederates. McKinney and several other Federals were marched sixteen miles barefooted. McKinney's prisoner then revealed that he was the leader of the Morgan squad that had captured him in 1864, and he had taken McKinney's custom made boots. After breakfast the prisoner offered to walk back to jail barefooted, but McKinney declined the offer.

On December 12, 1883, with McKinney still in office, the Board of Supervisors accepted the new stone jail. It was designed by Capt. G. I. Porter and was built of stone quarried at the lower end of the Moorman Ranch. When drilled and split with wedges, smooth blocks up to five feet long and two feet square were obtained for the jail walls. The new jail, 32 x 34 feet, was larger than the old one and contained four stone cells, 6 x 9 x 9 feet. The twelve-foot-high walls were two feet thick, and areas for wash and dining rooms were provided. The old wooden jail was joined to the stone structure, expanded, and made into quarters for the keeper. This fireproof and apparently impregnable structure set the stage for Sheriff McKinney's next adventure, one that neither he nor his daughter would ever live down.

In late September of 1884, John "Tex" Wilson stopped the Bodie & Lundy stage, soon after it had left Lundy, and abducted a Chinese woman whom he had learned carried money. He took her into the mountains, robbed her, and held her for eight days. Wilson, who went under many aliases, was rumored to have killed several men in Nevada, had kept a rendezvous for robbers near Candelaria, and was believed to have been involved in several stage robberies on both sides of the Sierra. His real name: Tom Kellett. In Lundy, he formed an alliance with several badmen: George Lee, and Jim and Charles Jardine. They virtually controlled Lundy at this time and enjoyed terrorizing citizens.

One evening in 1882, for example, Charley Jardine went into the Coblentz Store in Lundy, and, after a drink, drew his revolver and began shooting. Coblentz returned fire and both emptied their pistols; nobody was hurt. Jardine left and the door was locked, but he returned and fired two shots through it. Charley then had some words with Jim Hemmenway. Two hours later he had trouble with Moreno in Wilson's Saloon but could not get a gun. He appeared to have been beaten but carried a large dirk knife with which he cut Mike Delahide three or four times. Such was the crew that Sheriff McKinney was to face. Horse stealing was also a favorite of "Tex" Wilson.

Immediately after the stage robbery near Lundy, Deputy Sheriff Callahan tracked "Tex" through the light snow and captured him on October 3, 1884. He was taken to Lundy where, in the course of his examination, a shooting took place. Apparently holding some interest in the affairs of "Tex" Wilson, Ernest Marks of Bodie, and some Lundy friends, plied Charley Jardine with liquor, hoping he would kill off the prosecution's witnesses. Marks himself threatened the driver of the Lundy Stage, Andrew Waltze of Bridgeport; and Jardine, howling drunk, followed Waltze about Lundy, occasionally firing off his pistol in an attempt to provoke the driver, one of the most important witnesses.

"Tex" Wilson's attorney, C. A. Schuman, and Jardine had previously tried to start a fight with Sheriff McKinney as he stood on the porch of the Canyon House with his unshackled prisoner. While McKinney and Schuman argued, Jardine jumped forward with his pistol half-drawn from his overcoat pocket, his thumb on the hammer, ready to shoot the Sheriff and enable Wilson to escape.. Schuman was seized, and the Sheriff took his prisoner off to jail. McKinney manned the jail, fearing that some might try to free his prisoners, and had Deputy Sheriff Callahan patrol and secure the town. But the Jardine forces were bent on revenge, and when Callahan was in the act of arresting former deputy George Lee in Wilson's Saloon, the latter caught Callahan off guard and shot him, the wound eventually proving fatal. Lee was added to McKinney's garrisoned Lundy jail, but the night was not yet over before Kirk Steves and Jardine had wounded each other. The following morning, aroused Lundy citizens threatened to execute Lee, Jardine, and Wilson, and all prisoners were rushed to the new stone jail at Bridgeport. Jardine, later released, was killed at Bodie in 1890. "Tex" Wilson was quickly committed. Sheriff McKinney was commended by Ginn of *The Homer Mining Index* for his manly, fearless courage and was said to be a man of steel. He would need such qualities and praise for what was to follow.

On the evening of December 1, 1884, while awaiting trial, "Tex" Wilson escaped through the transom over the door of the stone jail. At about the usual hour of four o'clock, Sheriff McKinney failed to lock him in his cell. Then, working at odd times while the sheriff's daughter played the piano in their quarters, which were attached to the jail. Wilson cut through the transom bar with a knife blade saw and easily escaped in the darkness.

After the brash Wilson had returned to Mono County on several rustling raids, he was captured in Fresno County in September of 1887 and was jailed there. It must have been painful for Sheriff McKinney to read about the praise heaped upon the Fresno lawman who captured Wilson, and it must have been doubly painful to withstand the comments about his attention to duty and his daughter's piano playing, which many Bridgeporters said had driven the desperate Wilson to make his escape. "Tex", Baldwin, or Tom Kellett, as Wilson was variously reported, was said to have died at San Quentin in 1889; the same paper later reported his ten-year sentence to San Quentin in 1896 for robbing the Merced & Coulterville stage. He was definitely an experienced, clever criminal. Sheriff McKinney left office in 1887, and Watkin Morgan of Bodie was elected.

Like McKinney, Sheriff Morgan faced at least one unusual criminal. On May 30, 1885, at Coleville, Andy McGinty shot and killed William C. Barton. Governor George Stoneman offered a $300 reward, and McGinty was finally captured at Elko, Nevada, in early November of 1887. He had vowed not to be taken alive,

127

yet he surrendered and was tried at Bridgeport. Sheriff Morgan escorted McGinty to San Quentin to serve his seven year sentence. McGinty then published the following card in the *Bridgeport Chronice-Union* of January 13, 1888:

To the people of Mono County:

As I have been sentenced to State Prison for the term of seven years and six months, I deem it my duty to express my thanks to all that I have met in this county. I found the District Attorney to be a perfect gentleman, and the Honorable Judge also. I cannot express my thanks to W. O. Parker who kindly assisted me. I believe him to be a noble hearted man. And the Bridgeport jail I have found to be more like a home than a jail for the unfortunate. It is neat and clean in every respect, and our meals were well furnished and served so we could relish them. Our Thanksgiving dinner consisted of turkey and all the market could afford. Mr. Wat. Morgan, the Sheriff, furnishes the provisions for the jail and it is served by as kind a lady as I have ever met, Mrs. Wat. Morgan. Everyone is treated alike. My comrade has been a Chinaman. He has been very sick, but by good care and kind treatment he is much better without the aid of a doctor. Seven years and a half seems a long time to go to prison, but not having means to employ a lawyer or Jones to fall back on and being very downhearted, I thought it best to plead guilty to manslaughter. I am not a very healthy man but I hope to serve my term out for the sake of my dear children for they are homeless without father or mother to care for them.

Your respectfully,
Andrew McGinty

Sheriff Morgan was followed in office by another Bodie miner, M. J. Cody, in 1888. M. P. Hayes and E. E. Kirkwood, followed to finish out the century as sheriffs of Mono.

A Pioneer of California

The following narrative of Richard Gassaway Watkins extends far beyond boundaries of local history and presents a rare glimpse of an adventurer turned farmer:

I landed at Yerba Buena, now San Francisco, in the fall of 1844, from the U. S. man-of-war WARREN, of the Pacific Squadron. There were about half a dozen houses. From that time to 1846. I visited all the ports of California.

In June, 1846, the United States Pacific Squadron, under command of Commodore Sloat, was anchored off Mazatlan, Mexico, in company with the English squadron, commanded by Lord Admiral Seymour, the French Squadron, and a few men-of-war of other nations.

There was a banquet given on shore, by the British Counsel, to Admiral Seymour, and the senior officers of the other squadrons. Our vessels were anchored 5 miles off, and I was in charge of Captain Hall's gig that took him ashore to the banquet. They were having a grand time when a courier from the city of Mexico arrived with secret dispatches from the British Minister to the Counsel, advising him of the battles of Palo Alto and Resaca de la Palma, and that the United States had declared war against Mexico. He was instructed to notify Admiral Seymour to proceed forthwith to Monterey and take possession of California. In a moment all entrusted with the nature of the dispatch were unduly excited. Admiral Seymour ordered all aboard, and the British Squadron took a course apparently for Callao or Valparaiso.. An hour after the English Admiral had left table, Commodore Sloat gave orders for his officers to repair on board, the signal to get ready for sea was hoisted at the peak of the Flag Ship, and within a half-hour the American Squadron, under a cloud of canvas, stood to the north, and, by crowding sail and hugging the shore, arrived at Monterey on the 7th of July, anchored broadside to the Fort, and cleared for action. We landed, took

129

the Fort, and hoisted the American Flag—the first hoisted in California by legal authority. A few days after we had taken possession, I believe two, the British Squadron arrived, and the Admiral, chagrined at being outwitted and outsailed, at first refused to salute the flag. Commodore Sloat sent a Lieutenant with a note to the Admiral, reminding him of the neglect, and requesting an explanation—a salute was fired, but a coolness between both officers and men was the result.

The LEVANT and WARREN were dispatched to take possession of, and garrison San Francisco, and I was selected as one of the garrison.

There being no troops, the marines and sailors were organized for land service. I was attached to a cavalry company, and participated in all the engagements, including the relief of General Kearny at San Pasqual. While scouting between San Francisco and San Jose, we were attacked by Col. Francisco Sanchez, and, with five others, I was taken prisoner. We were stripped of everything except shirts, pants, and hats, and, after a brief council, marched to a clump of trees near San Mateo, and told to prepare for death, but while preparing to execute the sentence, a Mexican trooper dashed into camp with tidings that Chico Sanchez, brother of the Colonel, had been captured in San Francisco as a spy, and was to be shot to death. This saved us, negotiations being opened, with threats. A few days later the forces met on the plains near Santa Clara, and gave battle. Our squad was under guard on a sidehill in sight of the battle. The Mexicans were being driven back, when the notorious Three-fingered Jack rode up to the Sergeant of the Guard, with a verbal order from Col. Sanchez to shoot the prisoners, and join the battle, but he refused to do so without a written order. Firing ceased at sunset, and an armistice, until 10 o'clock next morning, ensued, when a parley was to be had. That night firing was heard in the rear of the Mexican camp, and their pickets driven in, the camp alarmed, and amid the bustle, the prisoners were hurriedly aroused, ordered to kneel, pray and prepare for death in five minutes; the squad detailed to shoot us was stationed about fifteen feet distant—did I pray? I did not swear—those five minutes were terrible. Suddenly the clear notes of a bugle sounded a *parley, and all were quiet; and at the campfire we were trying to thaw the chill of death from our bodies, as there was no more sleep that night. It appeared that Lieutenant Maddox, in command of a company of marines and sailors, anticipating a battle, had made a forced march from Monterey to cut off the retreat of the Mexicans, and came upon their advance pickets and drove them in. As soon as possible they were ordered to cease firing, and lay on their arms. That morning, when the fog lifted, both armies were seen drawn up in order of battle. A parley was had, and the Mexicans surrended. We then marched to Santa Clara and camped. A fandango was given, and the Mexicans and Americans vied in extending courtesies to each other, the only exception being Three-fingered Jack and a half-dozen of his like. As day was breaking, the reveille summoned us for early breakfast, and a day's forced march to San Francisco, where we arrived in the small hours of the next morning, and embarked on the U. S. Frigate SAVANNAH, Commordore Stockton, for Lower California.[1]*

Waktins reappears in San Francisco, arriving February 5, 1852, from San Juan Del Sur, Nicaragua,[2] having been a member of William Walker's expedition. Walker's attempt to form a republic in Nicaragua cost the young Watkins a leg but earned him a reputation from those under his command.[3] In 1859 the Washoe Excitement attracted him to Nevada Territory and placed him in location for what was to soon be "the most disasterous conflict to the whites ever raged in what is now the State of Nevada."[4]

Approximately three and one-half miles from Pyramid Lake in May of 1860, a reprisal force of volunteers from Virginia City and vicinities led by Captain Ormsby, was decimated, nearly obliterated, by Indian forces led by Chiquito Winnemucca. Captain R. G. Watkins, called upon to lead the Silver City Guards, had refused the leadership of the party because of his condition. But, there, strapped to the saddle of his powerful horse, he made several attempts to rally the men, as the Indian forces drove them into retreat and fired from both flanks along a low valley. After Capt. Ormsby had been wounded in the mouth and both arms, Watkins was urged to ride on, trying again to rally the fleeing men. No

1. *Bridgeport Chronicel-Union*, 2/28/91.
2. Rasmussen, *San Francisco Ship Passenger List*, Vol. III.
3. Thompson and West, *History of Nevada*.
4. Ibid., p. 158.

one was willing to resist, all were fleeing. Watkins returned to Ormsby who told him to save himself, and Watkins noted that within a moment "I was on my way to Carson."[1]

Watkins took up a man behind him and rode to safety and a place in the history of Nevada, the Battle of Pyramid Lake.[2]

As a result, perhaps, of such experiences we next find the Captain located in the yet remote solitude of Little Antelope Valley, in northern Mono County, where in 1869 he was well established on a 160 acre ranch complete with house. Somewhere between battles, the Maryland native had become an attorney; he served as a justice of the peace in Clinton in the 1880's and was, in 1896, Postmaster at Coleville; he also expanded his farming and ranching business into Antelope Valley. In 1888 the Folger brothers, his friends as well as proprietors of the *Bridgeport Chronicle-Union*, printed a notice stating that Watkins was among those entitled to a Treasury Department claim of $290 for service in the Piute Indian War. Ten years later and hard times in Mono County, the same paper noted, perhaps urging their friend, that Watkins had not yet been heard from as a claimant; perhaps the one-legged adventurer had put that memory aside.

In 1902, Watkins bought the Strickland (Farenbach) Ranch in Antelope Valley. He died in 1914. In addition to his valuable narratives of the Conquest of California, his Nicaragua experiences, and his narrative of the Pyramid Lake Indian War, Watkins, perhaps in suggesting yet another adventure, made a rather curious transfer of an interest in a flume and ditch to Eleanora Band— the consideration: "love and affection".[3]

1. Thompson and West, *History of Nevada*, p. 157.
2. Danberg, *Carson Valley*.
3. *Bridgeport Chronicle-Union*, Nov., 1880.

Men, boys, and dogs in front of the Simmons Saloon. The man seated on the high stool holding a dog is the proprietor, B. L. Simmons. Seated at Simmon's right is J. Murphey.

The Simmons-Loose Saloon

The Simmons Saloon, which burned in the fire of 1908, was originally located east of the old Allen House. In 1879, Wm. Loose purchased ground from P. G. Hughes and erected a handsome two story saloon, the Parlor Saloon. Loose had been elected Supervisor from Bridgeport and was very instrumental in Board of Supervisor decisions regarding the construction of the Court House; the Court Rooms for Department Two of the Superior Court were located in rooms above the saloon.

In Loose's saloon a difficulty occurred in which William Moore shot A. H. Stewart through the arm. Moore was tried in Justice Wild's Court, found guilty of assault, and was fined $40, Mr. Stewart refusing to make a complaint. This was the first fracas of its kind in town, and it occurred on May 15, 1880. It is also quite possible that the old building may have been built earlier than the 1879 purchase of land as C. E. Loose and A. E. Loose ran a saloon known as the Cosmopolitian in 1878. At any rate, Loose's saloon was moved uptown, in April of 1881, to the northeast corner of Main and Sinclair Streets, the site of the present Trails Restaurant. There it housed a number of saloon keepers: Loose, Fred Grimmer, C. B. Anton, "Pike" Richardson and B. L. Simmons. It was the largest of Bridgeport saloons.

133

This photo, circa 1880, shows the Loose Saloon building at its original location, the site of the present Union 76 Station. To the viewer's right is the old Severance Blacksmith Shop, one of the first buildings in Bridgeport. The Loose Saloon was moved to the corner of Main and Sinclair where it became the Simmons Saloon. To the viewer's left is what appears to be a small white rectangle, the roof of the Boone barn.

Big Springs
Election Fraud

The exact location of the "Big Springs" site of what has been termed one of the most glaring of California election frauds has never been accurately determined. It was September of 1861 and Aurora was still the County Seat of Mono County. The Supervisors at Aurora gave quasi-authority to some parties to open a polling place at "Big Springs" for the September Election of 1861, but there all traces on an election began and ended, even Davis and Orr, and Quint and Cavis, contestants for the Assembly and Senate, were not aware of the fraud. The motive remains a mystery, yet a list of 521 names as voters from "Big Springs" was made and counted at Aurora. These names were printed in the Legislature Reports of 1861-62. The list was later thought to have been made up in a cabin near Mono Lake.

The Assembly finally settled in favor of N. M. Orr against B. K. Davis, both residents of Tuolumne County. The Assembly case was between Joseph C. Cavis and Leander Quint. Judge Quint resided in Aurora, Cavis in Tuolumne. The Quint returns proved, after a Senate investigation costing $10,000, to be fraudulent, although it was nearing the end of the 1864 session before Quint was informed that he held office illegally.

Investigation showed that no more than twelve people lived in the area near Mono Lake, where the list of over five hundred names supposedly originated. A question put to one of the witnesses in the Quint case: Was there any loose sand about Big Springs, whereby the cabins, houses and tents could have been covered or buried during high winds, and all evidence of the inhabitants lost?"[1]

1. *Weekly Standard-News,* 4/27/81.

The Wild Man of Bloody Canyon

In May of 1882, the *Bodie Weekly Standard-News* reported that the Wild Man of Lake and Bloody Canyons was in town. It was his first trip out of the mountains since last December. He had grown much older in appearance since he was last seen, and his hair was nearly white. It was said that he lived in a cave. Upon this occasion he wore a huge overcoat made from the skin of a brown bear, a buckskin pair of pants, and a fur cap. This fierce looking individual always went heavily armed and talked as little as possible. He always had a few dollars when he came into town. Where he got his money and how he lived are mysteries no one had been able to solve. The reporter felt that it would be unsafe to insult him in his mountain haunts.

In March of 1883, Bodie again saw the presence of the Wild Man, but now some additional material came to light. His name was Tom Fitzsimmons, and he had come to Bodie in 1860 from Grass Valley. He prospected Bodie Bluff; then in 1869 he received news that his sister had died in the East. Since that time he had been a hermit, living in Bloody Canyon near Walker Lake and living on what he shot.

His bearskin coat of the previous year indicated his mountain survival abilities. Winter snow had driven grizzly and brown bears into Big Meadows. A huge grizzly in Bloody Canyon had been seen; its weight was estimated at 1,200 pounds. The fact that the Bodie bad men did not fool with the Wild Man would seem a testimony to this awesome individual.

Mining at 11,000 feet. The Ward village and the M. P. Hayes Co. Steve Kavanaugh and Hayes worked the summer of 1900 and struck promising ground. Kavanaugh Ridge lies above the cabin. The cabin is located just below the timberline.

Mining
at Eleven Thousand Feet

The accompanying photo showing three men in front of the log cabin was taken by Towle about 1900 and shows one of the several cabins of the old Ward mining village high on the northeast side of Dunderberg Mountain. In November of 1892, a four stamp mill had been built below the cabin to work ore from tunnels and shafts high above on the ridge forming the south wall of Green Creek Canyon. The mill was water powered, its four stamps crushing ore from the Ironsides, Bulkhead, and Castle Peak claims. Thomas Ward developed the property in the early 1890's, but by 1900 the property passed into the hands of M. P. Hayes and Steve Kavanaugh (the ridge above the cabin becoming known as Kavanaugh Ridge) who are standing in front of the cabin pictured.

It was always a small operation, but Ed Page continued to work the claims well into the 1900's. His tortuous trail from his cabin in Green Creek Canyon is still visibile from the heights of the ridge above; by using two long sticks as canes, Page pulled his crippled legs, by using his powerful arms, and was often crawling. The ascent was over two thousand feet, an almost vertical climb to the mineral deposits of the old Ward mines.

Charles Snyder, pioneer Big Meadows rancher and one of the organizers, in 1867. and discoverers of the Dunderberg mines. Snyder was an early rancher in Mason Valley where he joined the pioneers who had settled Smith and Mason valleys in 1859: T. B. Smith, R. B. Smith, S. Baldwin, J. A. Rogers, and later arrivals, W. R. Hall, D. C. Simpson, J. B. Lobdell, the Burbank brothers, and Daniel Wellington. Big Meadows ranching has been closely associated with that of Smith and Mason valleys. Photo courtesy Mrs. R. Snyder.

Castle Peak Mining District

In 1869 J. Ross Browne reported on the promising Castle Peak mines, which lay under and to the north-east of what is now known as Dunderberg mountain. Placer miners, who had worked Dogtown Creek, followed rich float up the creek to a granite and slate contact zone. The first discovery was made by Charles Snyder & Co., and a 40-foot shaft was sunk; three tons of ore hauled to Aurora, about 30 miles distant, paid over $50 per ton in gold and silver. The miners met at the cabin of Charles Snyder & Co. on July 10, 1867, and organized the district. Those present were J. S. Mayhugh, F. K. Bechtel, Charles Snyder, Fred Pollex, John Till, and Valentine Rock. The district began at the headwaters of Virginia Creek, south of Dunderberg, and ran north along the west base of the peak to the head of Green Creek, then east along the north bank of Green Creek to its junction with Virginia Creek, and then east and south to the point of beginning. The first locations were made on the ledge known as the Dunderberg, and the name was eventually given to the nearby mountain as there already was a Castle Peak nearby in the range. The Pioneer Co., Dunderberg Co., Castle Peak Co., Keystone Co., Thompson Co., and the Wirtenberg were among the first in operation.

Then, Dr. George Munckton and others, from Carson City, purchased the claims and formed the Munckton Gold and Silver Mining Company, which was in full operation by 1870. Dr. Munckton, a Carson druggist, had been one of the first to the Aurora strike and now invested heavily in the new property. The result was the exploration of the Dunderberg ledge via tunnels, the erection of a mill, and the development of a small town, Munckton. The camp of Munckton, perhaps the most obscure of Mono County mining camps, was in full swing during 1871-72, and was probably situated on the flat ridge below the mouth of the present tunnel. The saloon of Joseph Hutchins was a popular Main Street retreat. Also on Main Street was the two story Munckton Boarding House, which was sold to Summers and Samman in 1872. North of the boarding house on Main Street was the store of A. F. Bryant and Alex Scott, the latter serving as postmaster during the short duration of Munckton. Haight Street, a side street, was named in honor of Governor Haight.

By 1873 Munckton & Company had run a tunnel over 600 feet and had struck the ledge about 250 feet below the surface. The ledge ran north and south and was very wide, as their 34 foot crosscut had yet to strike the hanging, or opposite wall. They then drifted north and south for about 300 feet and found continuous quartz the whole distance. Ore was worked in the Levi Dague Mill, which had ten stamps of 650 pounds, but the presence of sulphurets and the rather low assay values soon led the company to bankruptcy. The mill was sold at Sheriff's Sale in 1872.

A. F. Bryant and G. K. Porter took over the mining property and, in 1878, after having been idle for about six years, they leased it to Ogg and Foote. Thirty men were put to work, and in July the mill whistle was sounded as they began crushing. Physical work was especially difficult at that elevation, the bottom of the tunnel was over 2,000 feet higher than the Main Street at Bridge-

A companion photo of the Dunderberg mining property. This one is taken from beyond the slum and tailings pond and looks southwest toward the ridge where the tunnels are. To the left is the mill; the building to the right is probably the chlorination plant. Above the snow atop the highest ridge is the property of the old Ward Mining Company described in Mining at 11,000 feet. Photo by J. W. Towle.

port. This operation also failed, and in July of 1880 the mill was dismantled and hauled to Bodie where it became the Silver Hill Mill.

The Dunderberg property then lay idle until 1891 when English capitalists became interested in the mines, repaired and cleaned out the tunnel, timbered it, and thoroughly assayed the ledge. A new track was laid in the tunnel in August of that year and several tons of ore were extracted and shipped to San Francisco. In 1895, the English interests bought the mine, and residents of Bridgeport looked optimistically to the business that the Mines Exploitation Syndicate would bring to the slumbering town.

The old I.X.L. mill, located at Silver Mountain, Alpine County, was purchased in 1896 and hauled to the new site. It had originally cost $60,000 to erect the mill at Silver Mountain, but it had never been run, so the new company had a new mill. The English syndicate soon became involved in a lengthy lawsuit with its representative, A. D. Cullum, lost the property, and Cullum took over as owner in 1899. the young and wealthy Englishman changed that name back to the original, Castle Peak, invested heavily, and put manager E. J. Andrews and superintendent Kermeen to work. Arrangements were made to run the mine all winter by constructing a tramway 500 feet long from the tunnel to the

A J. W. Towle photo taken from the ridge west of and looking down on the tunnels, buildings, boarding house, and mill of the Dunderberg mine. The older log cabin structures may be the remains of the town of Munckton. Note the long trestle for ore cars running from the main tunnel to the mill. Above the roof of the mill can be seen tailings and slum ponds. In the distance is the road to Bridgeport.

The remains of the four-stamp Ward Mill on Dunderberg Slope. Photo by H. M. Sain.

A photo by Frasher showing a portion of the stamp battery and mortar box of the Dunderberg Mill. The casting inscription and date is an example of that of many such mills built in San Francisco and illustrates how Mono County mining added to the economy of the City.

mill. The tramway was roofed and snowsheds and carpenter and blacksmith shops were erected. A cyanide plant was added, and a 75 x 86 chlorination works, complete with a 45 foot stack, was built in the fall of 1900. About 50 men were now employed.

In the journals of Clarence R. Wedertz we have an account of the daily work at the Dunderberg. In late January of 1896, Wedertz, Brown, Horan, and Rodgers were taken by sleigh, by James Logan, to within four miles of the mine, at which point they packed their bedrolls on a toboggan and began to walk. Rodgers gave out in wading through the heavy snow drifts and froze his big toe. Upon their arrival, Wedertz started the night shift as a driller, and work was rough. When they ran out of candles he carried the heavy box from Green Creek to the mine. Work was sporadic, and layoffs were frequent; in March he quit and walked all the way back to Bridgeport. He returned in July and got a job running the ore car, but the job that was the easiest was running the ore crusher in the mill. In October he was joined

142

by George Kirkwood in the mill. The mill shifts changed at noon, and Wedertz worked from noon until midnight; but heavy winter storms often forced operations to close. In November they kept a skeleton crew of 18 men as a telephone line was being put up to connect the Dunderberg office with Bridgeport. At the end of the month they shut down the mill, and he and George walked the 14 miles back to Bridgeport.

On his next shift at the mine, in December, he was put to work shoveling ore in the mine as the mill was still shut down. A new tunnel was started and Wedertz complained in his journal of the oil jackets necessary to keep one dry while working in the water they encountered. He soon returned to his old job at the mill, where he worked with three others. After his 12 hour shift he usually ate a few hot cakes, then slept until noon, got up, ate again, and talked a while. He then went back to sleep until five. The shift bell was rung at six o'clock, and after supper he took his lunch and walked to the mill. There they made coffee at one a.m. It was about 300 yards from the mill to the boarding house and it was a steep climb; the noise of the mill crushing ore made it difficult to sleep.

At the end of January there was great commotion in the camp; there hadn't been a payday for about six months, and everyone but the mill men had stopped work. Then, on the first of February, the miners sent three men to the Superintendent's office to ask if he would hold the bullion if the men were not paid. His answer was favorable so the men returned to work.

Wedertz continued to work when the mine offered employment, and in November of 1903 he noted in his journal that it took an hour and a half to change clothes because rubber suits were worn from head to toe. He worked 800 feet back in the tunnel where water came down in bucketsfull. He noted that it was hard to drill because the ground was very slippery and full of cracks and it caved a great deal. The drilling machine did not work well, and when it did it produced too much steam for them to be able to see anything. In December of that year the mine closed down for the winter, and the company made plans to drill a tunnel from Green Creek Canyon to tap the water and strike the ledge at great depth. This was started the following spring but was not completed.

The small cabin was just southeast of the present Sturgeon home at Bridgeport.

Snowslide ruins of the mill of the Par Value and Arnot Mining and Milling Co.
Photo by Corde Hays, courtesy J. Brandon.

Green Creek
Mining District

As early as 1880 Judge J. G. McClinton, and others from Bodie, discovered promising mineral deposits at the head of Green Creek Canyon, but it was not until the 1890's that capital from Bridgeport, Connecticut, was used to develop the ground. Charles Glynes and John J. Phelan were the principal Connecticut interests. In February of 1899 the property was incorporated as the Par Value and Arnot Mining and Milling Co. The Arnot claim being named in honor of Judge Arnot of Alpine County. A road had been built to the head of the canyon in December of 1898, and W. P. Brandon was hauling ore from the Arnot and Par Value claims to the Dunderberg mill.

In September of 1899, the company erected a Pratt Ideal Stamp Mill. A larger capacity Pratt Mill was installed in September, 1900, but during the winter heavy winds and snow crushed the mill. The property was soon abandoned by the company, but Frank Page, who had taken up a number of extensions around the Par Value and Arnot, continued to work the ground. Edwin Page built a cabin high above East Lake, a cabin later burned to the ground to supposedly keep people out of the area, and worked the claims for many years. Nearby Page Peaks, Par Value Lake, and Glynes Canyon are place names reflecting this mining ground and those involved. The two accompanying photographs, taken by Cord Hays, show the ruined mill amid snowslide evidence, and a cabin.

Ed. L. Page at the site of one of his last mining ventures. Drilling by hand through a granite-metamorphic contact zone on the Green Lake trail; the crippled Page often roped timbers around his waist and crawled on all fours to get them to the site. Note the hand windlass and the Cornish kibble ore bucket, basic mining. Photo taken in 1948 by miner Corde Hays. Courtesy J. Brandon.

Ed. Page wintered at the old Pedrocini cabin east of the East Walker. Note the stick canes and hobnail boots of the near hermit; the left knee shows several layers of patching. In younger days he wintered alone in a cabin he built above East Lake, miles from the nearest road and over 9,000 feet elevation. He once met a bear coming out of a tunnel he was working and killed the animal with an axe.

146

Doctor Clark Sinclair with his wife and two children, William and Flora. Photo courtesy Alice Dolan.

"Doc" Sinclair,
Sheep and the Poor Farm

On the evening of September 9, 1889, Doctor Clark Sinclair was sitting in his drug store, on the corner of Main and Sinclair, when Red Lee, a ranch hand who had worked the haying season at the Hunewill Ranch, staggered in and asked for some Magnesia. Lee was drunk, and as he sat conversing with the Doctor, he mentioned that he was a bad man and had just had trouble with a man named Simmons. Lee had about decided to go back and shoot Simmons. As he spoke he slowly drew his pistol and aimed it at the Doctor's chest; he cocked it and then deliberately lowered it and fired. The ball passed through the Doctor's left leg just under the knee joint, and Sinclair yelled that the shot had broken his leg. Lee insisted, in drunken logic, that he hadn't hurt him, and Sheriff Cody quickly arrived and arrested Lee.

147

The citizens were shocked over the brutal and senseless outrage, for "Doc" Sinclair was their only physician and was one of the most needed and popular residents of the town. He had arrived in the 1860's from his native Michigan and had taken up a small ranch. His wife was the daughter of Wentworth Calkins, a pioneer rancher who had about 600 acres in Big Meadows. Unlike physicians at other camps and towns, Doctor Sinclair had been very successful in treating Scarlet Fever and had lost only one case in the forty he had treated during an epidemic. Bridgeport could not afford to lose him.

The ball from Lee's gun had torn a large flesh wound, which the Doctor himself treated, but it did not heal. He spent a month trying various remedies and made frequent trips to Buckeye Hot Springs. Finally, in December of 1889, he went to Oakland where his left leg was amputated. He returned to Bridgeport and in May citizens raised money to buy him an artificial limb. He then continued his practice until he sold his Main Street property, purchased the old Goodall home just east of the present Bridgeport Hotel, and remained there until 1897 when he was appointed County Physician of Esmeralda County. This left patients in Bridgeport, Antelope, and Smith Valley without a doctor until Dr. Keebles filled the vacancy.[1]

"Doc" Sinclair had been one of the first in the sheep business in Mono County, having purchased a band in 1887, and this venture provided a prelude in violence to his later encounter with Lee. In August of 1887 Sinclair's son, Willie, left their sheep camp, which was six miles east of town on the Geiger Grade road, and told herder Jean Pratt that he would return that night. When Willie returned he could not find Pratt, and Sheriff Watkin Morgan, with a posse of whites and Indians, searched the area. Pratt was found less than a mile from camp in a pile of rocks and had been shot through the head. Governor Bartlett offered a $300 reward for the arrest and conviction of the murderer.

Willie Sinclair married Mary Green, of the pioneer family that had settled at Nine Mile. Then Willie joined in the rush to Tonopah, and by 1902 he was quite wealthy.

Doctor T. B. Keebles, of Bodie, had been appointed County Physician in 1890. He had served in the Civil War in the Rhode Island Light Battery, but wounds suffered during the battle of

1. *Bridgeport Chronicle-Union*, 4/12/90.

Antietam made him unfit for military activity so he was appointed a medical cadet in the General Military Hospital where he remained for 18 months. While in Mono County he was elected to the Assembly. Then, in 1898, he left Bridgeport for Yountville and administered the hospital there.

The County Hospital, which was established at Bodie in 1879, was very difficult to administer, and it was often investigated by the Board of Supervisors. When Bodie declined and the hospital was moved to a spot opposite the intersection of Highway 395 and the Green Creek road, the administration of the Poor Farm, as it was then known, remained a problem for the County. It became a refuge for the aged, ill and penniless. A cemetery was soon populated across the ridge behind the Poor Farm, and as tax revenues from the once flush Bodie and Lundy camps diminished to almost nothing, the Board of Supervisors complained of the cost of maintaining the facilities. In 1891, for example, the officials complained that the bills submitted at the last session were a curiosity, whisky and patent medicines predominated. The Board maintained that whisky might be a necessity but they felt that it should be bought by the barrel instead of by the bottle or glass. They recommended that patent medicines should have been bought by the case and pointed to the fact that one man drank four large bottles a month, and that was a medicine that was supposed to have been taken by the spoon. They also complained that tramps found the hospital a convenient layover.

One inmate of the Poor Farm, Peter Nye, occupied a room there for over seven years. He had been a master carpenter, and his career was smiliar to that of many who discovered nothing but frustration in the rush to follow the gold camps. Nye, a brother of the governor of Nevada Territory, was a pioneer of the Coast. He was a contractor in Gold Hill, and followed the rush to Aurora, where, in 1863, he declared his insolvency. He presented an unusual list of ventures that began with mining in 1850 in Tuolumne County. There he realized nothing above his expenses, and in 1851 he took up a ranch. The crop failed the first year; the second year he made about $5,000, but in 1853 he lost about $10,000 through floods and loss of stock. Teaming and lumbering looked good so in 1854 he tried that but made nothing. In 1855 Nye started a sawmill without capital and paid for the mill in lumber, but the mill broke down the following year, and that, together with bad debts, loss of stock, and property and lumber depreciation forced

149

him out. Nye came to Mono County in 1858 and engaged in packing, for wages, with J. M. Luther from Monoville, but he borrowed on his wages and fell behind about $700. Up until 1862 he continued to pack and trade for Luther by commission but made nothing.

When the County Seat was moved, he came to Bridgeport and became one of the chief builders; he helped remodel the old American Hotel when it was made to serve as the Courthouse. He built the Allen House and assisted in many other building projects, such as the erection of the Towle house. Then in 1874, a brother, Josiah Nye, purchased the ground just west of the river and south of the road from Thomas Kirkwood. Together the brothers erected a shingle and planing mill.

Then, in 1878, Peter Nye suffered a serious stroke that left him partially paralyzed. He never completely recovered and money was raised in Bodie and Bridgeport to help with his medical expenses. He suffered a second stroke in 1893 and was taken to the County Hospital, then still at Bodie. When the Poor Farm was completed he was moved there and remained in one of its small rooms until the end.

There were other carpenters, Adam Kidd, Jesse McGath, Dave Gilchrist, Thomas Sly, and Samuel Hopkins. Hopkins had learned carpentry and shipbuilding at the shipyard of H. M. Bean, Camden, Maine, and was a superior workman. He carried on the tradition and craft of his grandfather, who had owned a shipyard and was the first Commander-in-Chief of the Navy created by Congress at the outbreak of the Revolutionary War. Samuel served in the Civil War and then headed for California. Then, in about 1877, when Judge Leavitt was building his hotel, Hopkins arrived in Bridgeport and assisted in the construction. He built a fine residence on the corner of Main and Sinclair, just east of the hotel. This structure, a fine example of his carpentry, was recently torn down after the owner had offered it to the County. He also brought his fine craftsmanship to the erection of the Court House, and many of its intricate details and joinery are examples of his work. Before he died, in 1901, he had built fine boats for use on Twin, Grant, and Lundy Lakes.

Another contractor and carpenter, Charles B. Anton, was also a major hand in the erection of the Courthouse, and he maintained a carpentry and coffin making shop in town. The Anton home was just west of the Allen House in what was probably the old Dudleston home. Anton, like many others, was in the saloon business, but he sold out in 1886 to Fred Grimmer. The saloon was opposite the Leavitt House, but Anton was too busy with contracting work in the new Patterson District. He was, in fact, head carpenter for the Monte Cristo when that company began construction of its mill and out buildings in 1887. Anton moved to Fresno by 1890, so had Grimmer.

During the Bodie boom the town supported about six saloons that conducted a great deal of transient business; but when the mines collapsed in the 1880's the recession was extreme in Bridgeport, and the saloons were among the first to suffer as the small population of the town itself could not support them all, although several of the town's noted drinkers did their best to keep them all open. In early days it seemed acceptable for a man to undertake protracted sprees of at least a week or two, which were followed by brief intervals of sobriety. In this manner men from the outlying towns of Lundy, Cameron, or Bodie often entered Bridgeport with the sole purpose of spending a week or two in serious drinking. On such occassions, the local editors usually noted that the visitor was in town looking up old friends. Hank Blanchard and Lying Jim Townsend often made such visits from Bodie, and, in fact, did so much visiting and stretching of the truth that they were often unable to leave under their own power. Cowboys were, of course, especially prone to this diversion and it has come to be identified with their way of life.

Z. B. Tinkum, pioneer, lumberman, and public official. Considering the unusual birth of Mono as a county, it may be no surprise to find that Mono County Treasurer, Tinkum, held office while in jail. As Treasurer, Tinkum received $70 per month, the same pay as the janitor. He was requested by the Board of Supervisors, in 1881, to purchase all supplies and to do all work necessary to aid in the completion of the Courthouse. Tinkum later claimed to have received a $1,000 commission from the Supervisors for labor and materials he furnished. This action, perhaps in afterthought, was deemed a conflict of interests, and the same forces that employed Tinkum, jailed him until he was cleared. The fact that Tinkum served eight years as Treasurer seems a positive response by the public to his capabilities. He was born in Connecticuit in 1828, came to California and settled at Columbia in 1852; he was postmaster there in 1857. After Monoville in 1861, and sawmilling at Big Meadows in 1862-63, Tinkum lost his assets in the Aurora collapse. He then served as Mono County Sheriff before becoming Treasurer. He was very generous and left, on his death in 1894, thousands of dollars in worthless notes.

152

Sawmills
and Lumbermen

Lumbering was one of the first industries that the mining camps of Monoville and Aurora gave rise to. Sudden fluctuations in the economy of the mining camps was disastrous for owners of sawmills. Monoville and Aurora grew rapidly in the early 1860's giving rise to many competing sawmills, but there was a long period of economic depression between the collapse of Aurora in 1864 and the meteoric rise of the camp of Bodie in 1877. The Bodie boom created a huge demand for lumber, shingles, cord wood, and squared timbers used in crib work for shafts and in tunneling in Bodie Bluff. The heavily timbered slopes to the west of Bridgeport Valley were quickly claimed and steam powered mills were soon dotting what we now call Robinson and Buckeye creeks, and the East Walker River. Some of the first mills in Mono County were located on Mill Creek, in 1860, close by Monoville, the first population center.

The creek itself took its name from the several sawmills located there. About two miles above the mouth of Mill Creek was the Jones & Co. Mill. In 1861 Henry Clark, J. R. Jones, Cord Norst, and John Nichols held interests in the mill, the sawmill business being much like that of investing in mining stock. Also on Mill Creek was the mill of Thompson, Shed & Co. Two miles west of the Thompson mill, and six miles south west of Monoville, was Patterson's Pioneer Sawmill, operated by Robert S. and James H. Patterson. The latter mill property included seventeen yoke of oxen, three ox wagons, one mule wagon, 30,000 feet of sawed lumber, and one hundred and seventy thousand feet of logs in the woods on the heavily-timbered eastern slope of the Sierra, which drops sharply to Mono Basin. Otho J. Lundy, another pioneer lumberman, and Thompson remained in the area for some time, Thompson having an extensive timber land claim on Dunderberg slope from where, between 1860 and 1880, he supplied Aurora and Bodie with squared timbers and cord wood. The remains of two cabins can still be seen high on Dunderberg slope at what was known as the Thompson Wood Camp. The completion of the Bodie Railway and Lumber Company railroad and mill, in 1881, put many of the smaller lumber organizations out of business; the latter represented the peak of lumbering industries in Mono County.

The population shift from Monoville to Aurora in 1861, and the Aurora excitement, enabled those who had built sawmills in the timbered canyons around Bridgeport Valley, or Big Meadows as it was then called, to do quite well. The mill of Willard Whipple & Co. was located on Virginia Creek and was water powered. It had been in operation since November of 1861. Personal property included one log wagon. In 1864 C. R. Waterman acquired the property; in 1868 the machinery of the mill was stored at Bridgeport in care of J. W. Towle. It had been known as the Castle Peak Sawmill, one of the earliest.

Perhaps the first mill in operation near Bridgeport was Z. B. Tinkum's Tuolumne Mill Company, in operation in 1861, and located at the foot of Lower Twin Lake. In 1863 Tinkum built another mill below the old one and added double circular saws. In 1865 Sewell Knapp purchased the Tinkum property, which consisted of the sawmill, a shingle mill, lath mill, and dwelling house. The Moses Robinson and Hubbard mill was also in operation in 1861 and was three miles south of the Whitney & Co. ranch on what is now called Robinson Creek. They owned 1200 acres of timber land. Both Tinkum and Robinson operated mills on the same creek, Robinson's name being given to the creek as well as to a nearby mountain. Sawmill Ridge, above the creek, was aptly named. Robinson also lost out in the Aurora decline and in 1868 sold half interests in his mill to James Berry and M. Manning.

The mill and property of Roberts and Co. was located in Buckeye Canyon. In 1862, the mill became the Buckeye Mill Co. which went through the hands of Berry, Towle, and finally became the sole property of N. B. Hunewill. A second sawmill in Buckeye Canyon was owned by Mayberry and Hill. In 1879 they left a contract for 8,000 oxen shoes with a Reno blacksmith: two tons of iron. Such was the business during the Bodie boom. Hunewill also acquired their interests and in 1878 built The Eagle Mill, which ran day and night and turned out 30,000 feet of lumber per day and still could not meet the demand from Bodie and Bridgeport, although they ran three ox trucks of 36 oxen and employed 30 men. The manager was Jack Dennison. As many as

Jack Dennison, Clerk at the Eagle Sawmill in Buckeye Canyon. Dennison was a close friend of Dave Hays. Photo courtesy of Alice Dolan.

This photograph, circa 1875-77, shows the newly completed home of J. W. Towle and the old Nye planing mill, which was later remodeled as part of the old Wedertz home. Most of the trees in the area were planted after 1900. These are the present Huggans and Wedertz homes.

ten teams with 40,000 feet of lumber left the Eagle Mill for Bodie. A major problem, trouble with grizzlies at the corrals.

The mill of I. P. Yaney, in operation in the early 1860's was about four miles east of Fales Hot Springs on the Sonora and Mono wagon road. In 1869 Thomas Magilton acquired the mill, and about four miles west of it was a shingle mill. Yaney Canyon, by its name, suggests the activity of this early lumberman. In 1878 Yaney was Coroner at Bridgeport, and descendants now reside in Bishop.

Just north of Yaney Canyon, along the present route of Highway 395, is Patterson Canyon where R. S. and J. H. Patterson, who had the old Pioneer Mill at Monoville, acquired land in 1870 and built an extensive mill. In 1876 they sold to T. J. and J. E. Obenchain and S. Frost. The mill was seven miles north west of Bridgeport and included dwelling houses, corrals, barns, and steam boiler. The sale price included 150,000 feet of lumber. In 1878, future Mono County Sheriff C. F. McKinney had charge of the property, then called the Obenchain Mill. The mill, located at the mouth of Patterson Canyon, was destroyed by fire.

In the early 1870's, the Nye brothers operated a shingle and planing mill on the East Walker River at the site of the present Wedertz residence, the foundation and bolts still being visible.

155

An ox team and loaded logging truck, or wagon, typical of log hauling methods in early days. Photo courtesy J. Brandon.

In 1805

Transportation in its more primitive stages.
— In the High Sierras

A typical logging wagon, or truck, being pulled by oxen. The 12 oxen are yoked in teams of two and are chained together.

Two-foot long rounds were cut in Green Creek Canyon and floated down the river to the mill.

In 1890, Amos Green died at Green's Station at Nine Mile, Nevada, a station on the Carson-Aurora-Bodie route. He was the Green who had arrived with Whitney and Co. in Big Meadows, Green Creek bearing the family name. He was one of the pioneer lumbermen of the Pacific Coast and put up what may have been the first sawmill in the area at Sweetwater Canyon. In 1868 he retained 160 acres there.. His fine two-story squared stone home is still standing at Nine Mile. Mark Twain, then the young Sam Clemens, visited the Station on his famous journey from Aurora, during which time he and his partner lost their claim on what was soon the fabulously rich Wide West Mine.

Among the last active lumbermen in Bridgeport Valley was J. A. Hawks who, in 1894, bought the Montrose sawmill at Lundy, for use at his timber land about four miles east of Fales Hot Springs. His Last Chance Sawmill was so named because this was the only available timberland that he could find, and Bridgeport citizens hoped for another building boom. In April of 1894 the first load of lumber from the mill passed through town, the two teams being headed for the Standard Con. Mining Co. at Bodie. His competition was the Mono Mill and Lumber Company, complete with its 1881 raliroad.

Joshua West Towle and wife Adelia Wedertz. The couple had two children: Gertrude, who was County Treasurer and married Dan M. Smith; and Lottie, who married H. J. Bernard.

J. W. Towle

The land on which the old Towle home now stands was purchased from Thomas Kirkwood in 1874, a corral and stable then being the only structures. The Kirkwood ranch house was on the opposite, or north, side of Bridge Street. Joshua West Towle, born in Belfast, Maine, in 1832, was a lumberman who arrived in California in 1854. First Sacramento, then Sonora, Aurora and its rich mines finally luring him across the Sierra. He was soon in the Big Meadows, sawing lumber for Bridgeport, Aurora, and Bodie; the lumber used in construction of his own home came from the Buckeye sawmills where he and N. B. Hunewill jointly operated the mills.

Towle, like many others, suffered losses when the Aurora and Bodie excitements ceased, bringing about a virtual halt to the demands for lumber. During such periods, Towle held the following offices: County Clerk, Deputy Sheriff, Deputy Treasurer, Deputy County Clerk, and Assessor.

Towle had bought the old Yaney sawmill in 1870 and erected it in Buckeye Canyon. In 1875-76, he built the fine old Victorian home which stands on the corner of Main and Bridge Streets. Peter Nye, one of the chief carpenters in the construction of the home, was responsible for much of the detail work; Mr. and Mrs. D. E. Huggans have maintained the old home, complete with original furniture.

J. W. Towle home.

THE TOWLE HOME

In this photo, circa 1895, the condition of the house indicates the hard times that the collapse of Bodie brought. Standing at the left is Towle's mother-in-law, Mrs. L. E. Wedertz; to her left is her son, Frank L. Wedertz; then J. W. Towle and his wife Adelia Wedertz Towle. Standing on the ground with the carriage is Towle's son-in-law, Dan M. Smith, his wife Gertrude, and child, West Smith. To the extreme left is the old Wedertz home.

160

Patterson Mining District

This district is located on the east slope of the Sweetwater Mountains, about ten miles north of Bridgeport, and its close proximity to the County Seat resulted in a great deal of investment and excitement by local residents. The Bodie mines were in their decline just as the Patterson District mines began development, and, in the early 1880's, the County looked to this new discovery in hopes that it would renew the nearly disastrous state of the economy.

Prospecting in this district had been carried on sporadically throughout the 1860's, and rich float had been discovered. The source of the float eluded the miners until J. H. Patterson appeared. He had been attracted by something very peculiar to the area, the large quartz boulders found in Fryingpan Canyon. These boulders weighed several tons and yielded as much as $500 per ton in gold and silver. Finally Patterson, and Anthony Hiatt located the Discovery Lode on September 23, 1878, on the slope of Mt. Patterson. On September 21, 1880, J. E. Summers, J. H. Patterson, F. M. Cairn, A. W. McLean, and Joseph Thorp met, formed the district, and named it in honor of the discoverer.

The mineral bearing area lay to the east and south of the summit of the range, between Fryingpan Canyon on the south, and Sweetwater Canyon on the north. The vein systems are crosscut from east to west by deeply eroded canyons which allowed for exploration via tunnels and drifts. The veins occur in white porphyry and a variety of igneous formations are present. Of special interest are formations of banded rhyolite, andesite, and syenite. The best ore occurred in veins in irregular masses which were separated by low grade, (almost barren), quartz. There appeared to be three parallel mineralized belts, each separated by intrusive masses. These belts were termed the Cameron, Clinton, and Great Western. Ore at the south end showed a large proportion of gold, and ore at the north was almost exclusively silver bearing. As miners and speculators rushed to the new discoveries, three towns developed: Clinton, Cameron, and Star City. There also a settlement at the base of Mt. Patterson at Boulder Flat, directly above Star City.

161

THE CAMERON BELT

In 1887 the Monte Cristo Mining Company was incorporated with 100,000 shares that represented $1,000,000. The directors were Solon Patee, Washington J. Bevan, Daniel Buck, Alfred K. Durbrow, and W. C. Stadtfield, all of San Francisco. The Monte Cristo is located at the head of Fryingpan Canyon in the Cameron, or gold bearing belt. Other mines in this belt were the Patterson and the Thorobrace groups.

Prior to the incorporation, the Monte Cristo shipped its ore six miles to the Eclipse Mill in Cottonwood Canyon where assays varied from $35 to $200 per ton in gold. Early in 1886 Kilpatrick and Company, who owned the mill, moved it to Cameron, the town that had grown just below the Monte Cristo Mine. But the incorporation in 1887 allowed them to purchase their own mill, a Huntington, which was started up in August of 1887. C. B. Anton, of Bridgeport, supervised the construction.

By 1888, the Monte Cristo had spent $40,000 in development work, and a large amount of ore had been extracted from an open cut about 100 feet long. A tunnel had been driven in on the vein about 200 feet, and crosscuts and drifts were run. A crosscut tunnel was also being driven and, in late 1899, it was in 1900 feet, but they expected to run another 250 feet before striking the ledge. Three 8-hours shifts were at work.

The ore was hauled from the upper tunnel over a trestle 150 feet long and into the mill where it was reduced by a rock breaker and then automatically fed into two Huntington roller mills, each five feet in diameter. The heavy rollers pulverized the ore into pulp, which was then spread over amalgamated copper plates in sluices twelve feet long. The tailings were then run over blanket sluices 50 feet long.

This activity resulted in the development of the town of Cameron, located about one mile away, and named for Robert A. Cameron. An attempt to change the name of the town to Newburg failed, and in May of 1887 Tom Hill moved in several tons of goods and established himself as the first merchant. He had moved the old Gilson Building over from Bodie; in August he was appointed postmaster.

Teams from Bridgeport were busy hauling lumber and freight, and other structures were soon erected. In mid June there were six buildings which included Hill's store, John Huntoon's new saloon, a large boarding house, A. C. Raymond's dairy, and the stable of J. S. Cain and Vasey. The road to the new camp followed Fryingpan Canyon from its intersection with the Sweetwater road from Bridgeport. Cameron was dead by the end of the year, and the Monte Cristo continued to operate sporadically into the 1890's.

The Thorobrace Mine at Star City was one and a half miles west of Cameron by trail and was worked via two tunnels. A two compartment shaft, which cut the vein at 150 feet, was sunk and water was encountered. In 1884 a third tunnel was run to strike the vein 500 feet below the surface and to serve as a drain. In 1891, a rich strike was reported in the mine, but no other news followed. The mine and Star City were located on the divide between Fryingpan and Ferris Canyons. The Thorobrace had been originally located by Patterson and Hiatt in September of 1878.

Star City, like Cameron, had a short life, but in 1885 it looked so promising that the Folgers announced that they would publish a paper, the *Mono Record,* there; but this apparently never materialized. One of the largest buildings there was a boarding house kept by Mrs. Scott Summers, who had a number of boarders while the Monte Cristo operated.

THE CLINTON BELT

Above and to the north of the Cameron belt lay the Clinton group of mines, an argentiferous belt. In a draw, just north of Ferris Canyon, was the first and largest town in Patterson District, Clinton. In June of 1882 it consisted of about 40 buildings situated along a main street that ran east and west. Eben Trask's Livery Stable, Professor Hatfield's Tonsorial Parlor, James Compston's Hall and house, Laraway's Butcher Shop, Sheehan's Store, J. M. Campbell's Blacksmith Shop, P. C. Conway's house, the Borelin Bakery, Summers and Ebi's Boarding House, two assay offices, two saloons, a bootmaker, the notary office of R. G. Watkins, T. B. Brown's house, Mrs. Smith's Boarding House, several other residences, and a Chinese population constituted the town. John Sheehan served as postmaster. At the west end of Main Street, at the foot of the Sweetwater Mountains, was the five-stamp Summers Consolidated Mill. Ore, which then averaged $90 per ton was delivered to the mill on mules, which hauled from the Kentuck Mine located three miles above.

The Kentuck was the leading mine of the district, and its 30-40 foot ledge had been followed down over 200 feet by June of 1882. In one run of six days in 1882, the Kentuck produced over $2,000 in silver bullion at the company mill. The old mill had been brought over from Pine Grove, where it had been the Wilson Mill, but it was soon remodeled with a new 80 horsepower engine and a boiler from the Gold Hill Foundry. The old mill had turned out about $8,000 per month, and in September of 1883 the new mill was producing $19,000 per month.

But from its discovery by Page, Frost, Fullmore, Blake and Young, the Kentuck was involved in litigation which eventually caused the closing of the mine. The Summers brothers, who had grubstaked the discoverers, were sued by the discoverers, but in 1882 the court determined that the brothers were entitled to four-fifths of the property. This four-fifths was what formed the Summers Consolidated Mining Company, incorporated in 1883 with the following directors: W. Wright, J. N. Summers, A. D. Hunt, Martin Jones, and I. S. Hecht. The legal expenses had been heavy and one-fifth of the mine was sold to attorneys Bennett and Reddy for $17,000. Additional problems followed, the Summers brothers declared bankruptcy, the property appeared on the Delinquent Tax List of 1886, and it eventually became the property of John Sheehan who, in 1891, struck a promising body of ore. It was hoped that outside capital could be attracted, but at Sheehan's death in 1898, the Kentuck lay idle.

In 1884 the Summers brothers formed the Mineral Chief Mining Co., the capital being $15,000,000 in 150,000 shares at $100 each. The principal place of business was Bridgeport and trustees were R. M. Briggs, Z. B. Tinkum, A. F. Bryant, J. H. Patterson, and G. M. Summers. It was organized to work the Mineral Chief on which a double compartment shaft had been sunk over 200 feet. Assays were reported as being high and a tunnel was run to drain the mine of water that had been encountered in sinking the shaft.

This too failed, and in 1886 Henry Williams and others brought suit against J. N. and G. M. Summers and the Mineral Chief property, which consisted of the Discovery Lode and the Patterson mine; the property was sold at a sheriff's sale in May of that year.

The town of Clinton, however, remained alive until about 1891. In 1894 the Clinton School District was abolished. The first teacher was Miss Suttonfield, who opened the school in May of 1883 with 18 pupils. Miss Annie Dalzell soon took over as teacher. Clinton had been abolished as a voting precinct in 1892, and the town, which had noted its first death in the following manner, soon died also:

> A Chinawoman died at Clinton on Wednesday—As it was the first natural death that ever occurred there, the miners feel proud.[1]

Other principal mines in the Clinton Belt were the Lady Hayes, located on the north side of Mt. Patterson, and the Homestake, Poverty, and Silverado. The Lady Hayes was developed through two tunnels drilled through the south wall of Ferris Canyon, but by 1888 work had been abandoned. The Homestake had two ledges which crossed Silverado Canyon and was believed to be a north extension of the Kentuck. In the winter of 1891, the owner of the Homestake, A. P. Sayre, made a rich strike in a tunnel run in from Silverado Canyon, and the fact that the tunnel

1. *Bridgeport Chronicle-Union*, 1/4/84.

was run from the bottom of the canyon was a promising factor as the old Kentuck lay 2,000 feet directly above.

Connecticut investors purchased the mine from Sayre in 1901 and formed the Sweetwater Con. Mining Co.; John J. Phelan, of Bridgeport, Connecticut, was President. The Company purchased the Kincaid Quartz Mill at the old Kincaid mine in Nevada and erected the ten-stamp mill just below the mouth of the tunnel; in the spring of 1902 a cyanide plant was erected. The erection of their mill was delayed by a cloudburst which swept away many timbers and building supplies; even the rock breaker, an almost solid mass of iron weighing 5,200 pounds, was yanked down the canyon like a cork.

The Silverado was also a promising property, and was incorporated in 1884 as the Silverado Gold and Silver Mining Company, several Bodie residents being heavy investors.

THE COMSTOCK BELT

Above the Cameron and Clinton belts lay the Comstock series, located along the crest of the Sweetwater Mountains. The Comstock, owned by Doctors Deal and Anderson of Bodie, was one of the principal mines, but the Great Western group, owned by Henry Williams, was at the head of Sweetwater Canyon and proved to be more promising than the Comstock. August of 1891 marked the sale of the Great Western property to San Francisco capitalists who formed the Great Western Milling and Mining Company with a modest capital stock of $10,000,000. Directors were Martin Jones, William Irwin, H. C. Calahan, S. M. Booker, and Thomas Sharpe. William Irwin had been superintendent of the Standard Con. mine at Bodie during its prime, and the other directors were also men of Bodie experience; their interest in these mines lent credibility to the venture.

Further activity in the Patterson District was confined to the silver mines of Silverado Canyon and the Sweetwater Con. Company. Operations continued into the 1920's with the completion of a power line from the dynamo at Green Creek to Silverado Canyon. Eastman was Superintendent at the time and the writer's uncle, Robert Sawyer, was assayer. The output of the district from 1880-1888 was estimated at $500,000, $450,000 having been produced by the Kentuck.

166

The Bryants

In July of 1880 Amasa F. Bryant and wife donated a lot for the construction of the Courthouse. Such donations and involvement in public and community affairs have been characteristic of A. F. Bryant and his descendants since his arrival in California, from Boston, in September of 1849 on the ship *Regulus*.

In following the rush to Aurora, A. F. Bryant was attracted to the nearby Big Meadows, and there, in the fall of 1863, built the first store, a 16 x 24 foot building located near the East Walker River on the south side of Court Street. By 1866, Bryant had built a larger store, at the site of the present Jolly Cone and Bank of America on the north side of Main, the two story general merchandise building and residence remaining until fire destroyed it in 1963.

Bryant's Store on Main Street at the site of the present Jolly Cone; the picture was taken about 1897 and shows the building rigged for the Fourth of July. It was a common practice, brought over by miners from Europe, to cut saplings with which to line the streets. The Fourth of July was apparently close enough to ancient spring rituals for the sapling cutting and the July holiday to become mixed. Standing at ground and lower porch level from the viewer's left are: Charles Hayes, unknown, Harry McCall, A. F. Bryant, Mike Waltze, unknown, and Jennie (an Indian woman hired to help care for the children.) On the top porch are, unknown, Annie McCall. Photo courtesy M. A. Bryant.

Bryant's Hall after its removal to Emigrant Street.

At this time, about 1868, Bryant's Store and property included an adjoining ranch of 160 acres, much of the ranch land now forming the north side of Bridgeport. The old ranches of Bryant and Kingsley constituted a major portion of the present townsite of Bridgeport, and the two men were largely responsible for laying out the site. Bryant's involvement in the growing young county was prolific and included ownership of the Dague Mill at Castle Peak (Dunderberg). He had the mill moved to Bodie where it became the ten stamp Silver Hill Mill. He was one of the men behind the construction of the East Walker River and Munckton Toll Road in 1870. He opened a large store in Bodie, ran it during the boom years and returned to his Bridgeport store in 1881; Bodie citizens openly expressed their regrets at his leaving. In addition, he was the first Postmaster of Bridgeport and served for twenty-four years.

In 1884 Bryant erected a large public hall, which was located on the corner at the site of the present motel of M. A. Bryant. The structure had originally been the old Glynn Dale Hoisting Works at Bodie. Bryant's Hall, as the structure came to be named, was erected by G. L. Porter, Anton, and Sam Hopkins. A curious feature of the Hall, and a feature that added excitement to roller skating and dancing, was the placing of heavy leaf springs under the floor. The large 55 x 50 foot Hall was a popular social center for many years. In 1936 it was moved to a lot on Emigrant Street just east of the Church. In 1946 it was torn down. In the old days, residents had crowded the hall to see such traveling acts as magicians, musicals, dramas, acrobats, and small circuses.

168

In this photograph of Bridgeport from about 1900 can be seen, from the viewer's left: the Jesse McGath home, Bryant's Hall, the Courthouse, the Courthouse Corner Saloon, the two story Severe brick building, the two story Simmons Saloon. Beyond Simmons Saloon are smaller buildings comprising the fire house, Dr. Kerb's Office, Brown's Store, at least one saloon, then the larger buildings of Bryant's Store, the Allen House, Hughes' Blacksmith Shop, the Stanton building, and a portion of the J. W. Towle residence at the extreme right corner. Note the grass and sagebrush in the foreground on Main Street. At this time, the main road north-south passed between the Courthouse and Bryant's Hall. There was still no fence in the front of the Courthouse. Water for the Courthouse was still provided from a well drilled in the yard in August of 1880. A Forrester non-freezing pump was used to pump water to the large tank on the roof. Photo courtesy M. A. Bryant.

In 1897 A. F. Bryant's son, Amasa S., married Nellie Anne Sawyer at Bridgeport; in 1899 he took over the store, stock, and business of his pioneer father. The store remained in operation by the Bryant family until fire struck.

Amasa S. became a pioneer in another manner in that he pioneered in electricity and telephone line construction, having run lines to the Dunderberg Mine (some of the telephone wire was strung along available fence posts), Aurora, and Bodie, so that Bridgeport became a center for communication from the outlying camps. Poles, when used to string wire, were often slender willow poles; repair work on the lines during winter storms was dangerous work. A. S. Bryant died in 1943, aged 67, and left his widow, two daughters, Cora and Jean; two sons, Merrick, and Murven, the latter being the remarkable proprietor of Slick's Court. The Bryant family interest in the development of the community extended to donations of land for the present airport, Bryant's Field, and land on which the Catholic Church stands.

169

This photo by J. W. Towle shows the two buildings located on the site of the present Pembar Garage opposite the old Leavitt House. Here, in 1893, Mrs. Hayes set up the post office in 1893, the sign being over the door on the unpainted building. In August of 1897 Mrs. Chas. Calvin and child arrived and set up a residence in the dwelling adjoining the old post office. Mr. Calvin was bookkeeper at the Dunderberg Mine. The dwelling had recently been occupied by the then District Attorney Charles L. Hayes. Both structures were destroyed in the fire of 1908. The unpainted structure, known as the Crowell building, had housed a store.

Postoffice

A. F. Bryant, who had worked in the Boston Post Office and had started in the San Leandro Post Office in the early 1850's was Postmaster at Bridgeport for twenty-four years. He held the office from 1863 to 1887 when a change in Washington administration allowed for the appointment of Dave Hays. Hays remained in office until 1891 when Bryant again took over, enjoyed his victory, and resigned. In 1893, Mrs. Ella Brady Hayes took the office as Postmistress and set up office in the Crowell Building, opposite the Leavitt House. Minnie Pimentel succeeded Mrs. Hayes in 1897, and, in 1899, bought the old two-story Severe Brick building on Main Street and moved the post office there.

Mail carriers McTarnahan, George Moyle, R. Gelatt, and others had tough winter schedules. The railroad to Hawthorne, Nevada, completed there about 1882, provided for the mail to be carried by train to Hawthorne and then by wagon to Bodie and Bridgeport, thus avoiding the longer road route from Carson City. It was, in the 1890's, still not an easy route, as the following relates: "The mails—the big storm delayed the mails between here and Bodie, the stage not being able to come through Thursday evening. Sam Smith with a four-in-hand went out yesterday morning to meet the mail from Bodie and got as far as the hill above Morman (Moorman) Station, where he was met by George Montrose on snowshoes with letter mail only. On Thursday night the stage from Bodie got to the top of Booker Flat Hill and was compelled to turn back on account of the severe blizzard."[1]

---

1. *Bridgeport Chronicle-Union,* 4/10/97.

Strange Adventures
of Louis Samman

One of the pioneers of Dogtown and Monoville was Louis Samman, a native of Hanover, whose strange adventures eventually led to his death. The irony of Samman's death is based in a story that he circulated as a hoax in 1880 in a Bodie newspaper. In the article Samman told of how he had, several years previous, put three Indians in Mono Lake and that they had become petrified. He stated that he had intended to let the bodies remain about six months longer, at which time he could expect perfect petrifaction. He planned to send one to the Academy of Sciences at Philadelphia and another to the Medical Museum at San Francisco. The Bodie reporter noted that Louis was a queer fellow and delighted in the fact that a New York Newspaper had clipped and printed the article as another factual account of strange Western fancies.

Samman was one of the first to settle at the placer mines and claimed to have arrived in Yosemite in 1851, where he hunted game. He recalled that he was there when Hutchinson and his wife entered the valley. Then, in 1856, Samman crossed the Sierra to Mono Basin; he remembered that Von Schmidt had been busy running the Mount Diablo Meridian, and Samman kept busy hunting antelope, which were plentiful in early days. He stated that the first mining was done at Dogtown and that Cord Norst was among the first there. Samman remembered Lee Vining and the fact that Lee Vining Creek, once called Rescue Creek, was named after him and that Vining had the best claim at Dogtown. As late as 1868, Samman owned a small house on the trail from Dog Creek to Mono Lake; he too followed the rush to Monoville and then moved on to Bodie where he placered for gold in the early 1860's.

Samman also recalled that Bloody Canyon was a favorite route to Monoville and that a packer named Brookman ran a pack train from Big Oak Flat to Monoville via Bloody Canyon. A Monoville adventure that stuck with him was his witnessing a ruffian taking a shot at storekeeper C. W. Mills and watching

172

with amazement as the ball passed through the storekeeper's clothes without injuring him.

Samman's headquarters were at Mono Lake, and he had taken a ranch on the southwest side near Rush Creek. There he raised horses, butchered cattle, and kept a small store for Indian trade. He rather quietly worked his ranch and traded with the Indians for several years until January of 1889 when news of a murder reached Sheriff M. Cody at Bridgeport. Louis Samman had been murdered by Indian Jake, who also shot and wounded an Indian woman. The Sheriff organized a posse of five men and searched the area, but, for several days, Cody was unable to find his man until, after threatening and coaxing nearby Indians, Jake was brought forth.

Jake claimed that it was a case of self defense and that Samman had threatened to shoot him. So, Jake went into Samman's Store, got a shot gun, and killed the man. He described in detail how he shot Samman twice to make sure he was dead, but Jake was very reticent about his shooting of the woman. Jake claimed to have shot Samman outside the store and then dragged him in and onto a bed. Insiders claimed that Jake had caught Samman in bed with the woman, but the woman would say nothing, and the suspicions were never verified. It was known, however, that Samman had previously beaten Jake. In addition, Samman had threatened to kill his own wife and family, and, at the time of his death, the case was before the Superior Court. Soon after his death Louis acquired the reputation of having been a badman, and many recalled his so-called hoax, which now appeared in a chilling light.

One Bodie reporter mentioned that Samman had the reputation of having killed two men, whose bodies he had thrown into the lake. The lake, Mono, was for some time previous to the German's death, known as Samman's Graveyard. Also, in the 1860's an Austin, Nevada, paper referred to an incident at Mono Lake in which white pursuers had driven Indians into the lake and shot them. However fictional these accounts may have been, Bridgeport expressed great sympathy for Indian Jake; and his attorney, W. O. Parker, succeeded in an appeal to the court for mercy: the sentence for Jake was nine years hard labor at Folsom, quarrying stone.

173

Stacking hay at the Stewart ranch. White bearded Charles M. Stewart at viewer's left. Photo by J. W. Towle.

174

White bearded Barney Peeler. In 1878 he was badly hurt; the result was the amputation of his right arm. Barnabus, or Barney, is the namesake of the two Lakes Barney and Peeler, both above Twin Lakes. He was a stock raiser and was in partnership with Jesse Summers. Both left Missouri for California and may have come to Mono county together. A brother, Henry Peeler was also in Big Meadows but later returned to Missouri. Barney died in 1920. Photo courtesy M. A. Bryant.

Cattle Barons and Hay Crops

In 1864 Charles and John Russell sold their property in Russell's Valley to Jesse N. and G. N. Summers, who had driven their cattle north through Owens Valley to the Monoville area. The Russell property included four hundred acres on the tributary of the Walker River. The land had been surveyed for the Russells in August of 1861. Along with the property, the Summers brothers acquired one ox wagon, wooden axletree, mowing machine, horse rake, hand rake, and two thousand posts. It was not long before Russell's Valley became known as Summers Meadows, the tributary noted above soon bore the name of Summers Creek.

By 1868 Jesse Summers & Co. owned 640 acres east of Luce's Ranch and another 640 acres adjoining the above, the latter known as the old Davis Ranch. The property included the old Valley View Ranch, now called the Point Ranch. These large holdings which the Summers worked together with Barney Peeler allowed them to be able to capitalize on the huge demand for beef during the Bodie boom of 1877-83.

Jesse, a native of Kentucky, came across the plains in 1850 from Missouri, arriving at Nevada County and then on to Monoville in 1861. His brother, Dr. G. N. Summers, built the Grand Central Hotel in Bodie and was for a time in charge of the County Hospital which was then located at Bodie. The Summers Company owned five meat shops during the Bodie boom, operated a large slaughter house there, and enjoyed a virtual monopoly in the meat business. Jesse and his brother later became involved in mining, and as a result of heavy investing in the Summers Con. mine and mill at Patterson District, in the Sweetwater Mountains, they lost their possessions in 1885. Jesse moved to Oregon where he regained investments, re-established himself, and was doing quite well until his death at Linkville in 1890. G. N. Summers had moved to Fresno, where he died in 1892, having practiced medicine for nearly 55 years.

The end of one empire, that of Summers & Co., began in June of 1883 when Jesse Summers sold 10,819 acres in Long Valley and Mono Basin to Kirman and Rickey. At this time Kirman and Rickey also bought meat markets at Bodie and quickly established themselves as successors to the Summers cattle empire.

The Rickey empire began in Antelope valley in the 1870's with Thomas B. and Henry, sons of William Rickey, Thomas becoming the cattle baron of the family and valley in his partnership with Richard Kirman. In 1880 it was reported the partners, quite active in establishing new grazing land, had Chinese digging a ditch in Antelope Valley. Soon they acquired interests and ownership in the Walker River Irrigation Ditch Co., the Tunnel Ditch Co., and the Hartshorn Ditch. Control of water and the building of new ditches enabled Kirman and Rickey to control land. In 1882 they began acquiring land very quickly in Antelope Valley, buying out the smaller ranches of Swauger, Moore, and Cochran, which gave them the greater portion of the valley. A gang of Chinese under their direction had cleared off sagebrush in the upper end of the valley and alfalfa was then planted.

In 1883 the blackleg killed a number of cattle, and bears roaming between the Little Walker and West Walker Rivers were killing livestock. By 1884 T. B. Rickey was well known as the cattle king of Antelope Valley, and in April of 1885 a post office was established at Kirman and Rickey's ranch headquarters in

176

Antelope Valley and was called Topaz. Walter Swart was post-master.[1] The ranch headquarters became quite a settlement, a true-ly Western cattle camp. In December, 1888, Topaz continued to grow when the company erected a large two-story boarding house, built in the shape of an "L". Included in the building were two large dining rooms, one exclusively for ranch employees. In the rear was a large ice and store house. Plans included the erection of a stable and the planting of orchards.

Meanwhile, Kirman and Rickey had over 3,000 head of cattle at the old Summers ranch above the Point. There the partners had a large platform scale to weigh cattle. In 1890 they drove at least two thousand head from the Point Ranch through Bridgeport and on to Antelope Valley where they wintered the cattle. By 1892 Kirman and Rickey had bought the old Morris Dick ranch at Antelope and the one thousand acre Waltze Dairy Ranch at Bridgeport and were leasing the old Huntoon ranch while they battled foxtail grass, which had invaded the valley in 1889 and had ruined most of their Antelope Valley hay crop. Also, they had, in 1889, purchased 21,000 acres of School Land in Lyon and Esmeralda counties. The market for beef was no longer in the nearly dead camps of Aurora and Bodie. Now they shipped cattle to San Francisco via the railroad at Carson City. In 1892, for example, they shipped eleven car loads.

In 1895, Rickey Ditch in Bridgeport Valley, was constructed when Kirman and Rickey brought in and used a twenty-horse

1. *Bridgeport Chronicle-Union,* 4/11/85.

ditching machine. Water was always the key issue, and the building of the Rickey Land and Cattle Co. came with at least two hard fought water suits, the first in 1888, but both involving cattlemen.

The first suit saw Kirman and Rickey pitted against pioneer cattleman N. B. Hunewill, the latter having turned placer miner in this case. Hunewill held a placer claim, the Rancheria, at the old Mono Diggings. He claimed possession of Ditch No. 1, the old Mono Diggings placer mining ditch which headed from the west fork of Dogtown Creek at the Thompson Wood Camp on Dunderberg slope, having been part of the old double ditch system dug in the summer of 1860.

In April of 1887, Hunewill leased the water from the ditch, the water of which he had diverted across the divide to Mono Diggings, to D. E. Jones and the Virginia Creek Hydraulic Mining Co. The plaintiffs claimed, in their 1888 suit, that they were wholly deprived of water for four months at the Point Ranch. The suit was decided in favor of the plaintiffs, Kirman and Rickey, by Judge O. F. Hakes who argued that the natural flow was through Virginia Creek and through the old Valley View ranch.

"The Big Meadows hay crop will be about 10,000 tons— not a good year." 8/25/88 BC-U.

Richard Kirman died in 1896, Kirman Lake above Leavitt Meadows bears his name. In 1897 T. B. Rickey reportedly bought out the Kirman interest and continued the cattle empire on his own. Kirman, a native of England, left an estate of $500,000 and had been with Rickey over twenty years.

"T. B. Rickey has cut everything that wears grass." 9/23/99 BC-U.

In 1899 T. B. Rickey began a project that was to involve him with the greatest of cattle kings, Miller & Lux. The Rickey plan was to convert what was then Alkali Lake in Antelope Valley into a reservoir. Rickey owned the lake-bed, which was ¾ of a mile wide and 2½ miles long. In addition, Rickey had water ditches running to the lake bed from the West Walker River. The plan called for a lake about thirty feet deep and about one hundred acres in area. His plan included selling water to farmers and ranchers in Smith and Mason valleys. It was this latter aspect of the plan that concerned Henry Miller, who had ranching interests in Smith and Mason valleys. Furthermore, Rickey claimed riparian rights to all the water on the California side of the State line; the fact that the water originated in California and was used in Nevada complicated the issues. The case involved at least 160 defendants and was finally resolved at the Supreme Court level in favor of Henry Miller.

Miller then agreed to the construction of the reservoir with the condition that all parties be supplied with water.[2] Water was also behind the several attempts by the State of Nevada to have the boundary between California and Nevada fixed at the crest of the Sierra rather than its present and somewhat confusing boundary.

"The farmers have finished haying for the winter."
9/11/97 BC-U.

About 1906 the Rickey Land and Cattle Co., managed by C. W. Rickey, remained the principal land owner in Antelope Valley. Thomas had begun buying in 1876, and now the ranch consisted of 35,000 acres. The company's hotel, stores, residences, and ranch buildings, including a jail, formed the major portion of the town of Topaz. But Rickey lost heavily in Tonopah in 1907 and the empire dissolved.

Other ranchers, G. B. Day, D. C. Simpson, and Charles Snyder only recently left Bridgeport Valley, some locating in Smith and Mason valleys, the descendants carrying on the business of ranching. One of the first of the ranching families remains, that being Hunewills who celebrated a centennial in Bridgeport Valley in 1961. There, on the original ranch of N. B. Hunewill, cattle are yearly raised, then wintered at their ranch at Smith Valley.

The sheep raising industry, which got underway in Mono County in the mid 1880's, soon created heavy demands on space and grazing area as huge bands were driven up from the San Joaquin. In May of 1887, Miller and Lux had seven thousand head, M. Brazil had 1,500, and the Condozas had four flocks; there was no feed on the other side of the Sierra. It was not uncommon then to have bands of two thousand sheep driven through Bridgeport.

In an attempt to gain control and revenues the County enacted sheep and cattle licensing ordinances. In 1891, almost $10,000 was collected; in that same year C. C. Turner drove a

1. Treadwell, *Cattle King*, pp. 105-110.

The handsome Latapai family who took over the Huntoon Station and property, prime sheep country.

band of 2,000 head through town to the Old Waltze ranch. In July of 1895, almost thirty thousand sheep were sheared at Huntoon's.

One of the sheepman's foes was the coyote, and with increased bands and flocks, along with pressure from the sheepmen, the County passed a curious act. After March of 1891, any person killing a coyote was entitled to five dollars. This was called the Coyote Scalp Bounty Act, and one enthusiastic Antelope Valley hunter deposited 27 scalps, which included the noses, in the County Clerk's Office. In July of 1894 the County Board of Supervisors burned 61 coyote scalps and paid out $305.00.

In the fall of 1899, the act was repealed; the local editors felt that the payment should have been reduced, not repealed, since coyotes appeared to have multiplied.

Before the major ranchers, like Hunewill, had developed winter ranches in Smith and Mason valleys, it was a common practice for some of them to move into Bridgeport for the winter. In such a case James Sinnamon and Norm Huntoon were reported to be moving into town in November of 1895, the ranches being left in charge of employees.

The short seasons, the cold winters, and the elevation all combined to form a short growing season, hay being the only crop grown on a large scale in Bridgeport Valley. Valleys of lower elevations in Mono County and in Nevada provided a climate for the growing of crops and orchards in abundant variety. Even at Mono Basin, near the base of Bloody Canyon, farming was much more successful than in Bridgeport Valley. In August of 1881, for example, the King Ranch owners had cleared nearly five hundred acres of sagebrush in the past three years. They had eight hundred fenced acres, had cut four hundred tons of hay, had thirty-five acres of potatoes, sixty acres of oats and barley, and two acres of cabbage. The volcanic soil was especially good for vegetables.

The only seriously successful raisers of vegetables in the vicinity of Bridgeport Valley were the Chinese, who kept gardens in their village at Clark Canyon and on the edge of Warm Spring Flat. The produce was peddled in Bridgeport.

Bancroft collected the following information in regard to Mono County:

In 1867—very little has been done in the County in the line of farming—the amount of land inclosed having been about 6,000 acres. In 1876—there were 21,578 acres inclosed . . . 25,000 cultivated. Products in 1876: 100 bushels of beans from 2 acres, 500 bushels of wheat from 25 acres, 4,000 bushels of barley from 200 acres, 500 tons of potatoes from 200 acres, 15,-000 tons of hay from 15,000 acres, and 500 pounds of honey. In the county there are 2,500 horses, 100 mules, 11,000 horned cattle, 10,000 sheep, 1,200 goats, 750 hogs, and there were 50,000 pounds of butter churned. There was one water-power grist mill that made 100 bushels of flour. Also among the improvements were 100 irrigation ditches worth $10,000 and used over 15,000 acres that were valued at $45,000.[3]

3. *Bancroft Scraps,* 1877, p. 407.

Sheep dipping at the hot waters of the travertine was an extensive operation.

Deadman Summit and Creek

For those who have traveled Sonora Pass and noted, perhaps curiously, a rushing stream known as Deadman's, which passes through angular granite walls, events have been passed on to explain the naming of the creek and crossing. When the Dogtown placers were being worked, a prospector left Sonora in June of 1858 for Mono. He was well outfitted, but no one, apparently, knew his name; some noted that he was well educated and, spoke several languages, and felt that his name was Joseph Madison. Nothing was seen or heard of him until October of 1859 when his remains were found at Deadman's Crossing between two huge logs about two hundred feet from the trail. The body had decomposed, but the head had been covered with an overcoat. The four-man party that discovered the body found several letters and papers, one which addressed him as William Barrett. Over sixty dollars was found in a pocket, a camping outfit was found nearby, and conclusions confirmed a natural death had occurred. No horse or pack animal was found, however. The crossing and creek further established its name in 1860 when the body of a sheepherder was found near the same spot; in 1868 another body was found at the crossing.

Buckbee reported that the area may have been named for two Mexicans who packed between Sonora and Aurora for George McQuade and whose bodies were found. Murder was suspected as the two were thought to have been carrying gold.

Another account relates that a man enroute to Sonora stopped at Leavitt's, at the eastern base, and Leavitt tried to pursuade the traveler to stay over as it was storming. His body was found the next day by Dave Hays. It was the winter of 1861 so Hays and Leavitt buried the body in snow; in the spring they dug a shallow grave along the river, Deadman's River.

Prof. Clay Hampton and Addie Donnel, standing at rear and right of center, with a circa 1890 class of Bridgeport's finest. As can be noted, the girls were carefully separated from the boys so as to not interfere with "learning". Photo courtesy M. A. Bryant.

School

From earliest days, residents of Big Meadows provided formal education for their children, the first organized effort being at the instruction of Charles Elliott in the early 1860's. This was done at private residences. The Elliott involvement in education was extensive; W. F. Elliott was Mono County Superintendent of Schools in 1879.

The *Esmeralda Union* of December 14, 1867, related that Rebecca Poor had begun teaching public school at Bridgeport and that they had long needed a school. Finally, in August of 1880, the school house, now used as a museum at its new location, was opened; one-armed Barney Peeler had donated the bell. Miss Carrie Havens of Oakland was the teacher, and the school census, conducted that June, showed 116 children in Bridgeport District. There were 43 children under five years of age and 118 between five and seventeen. In 1896 there were only 66 children, fifty of whom were school children, a substantial drop and another indication of the near poverty level of the Bridgeport economy.

Among the most popular of Bridgeport school teachers were Prof. Clay Hampton, who taught from 1886 to 1892 and then

This photo shows the old Bridgeport School located at the head of School Street. A careful look at the gate in the fence shows a wooden turnstile, later removed by student pranksters. Another trick, recalled by M. A. Bryant, involved the dismantling and assembly of a wagon, the latter operation taking place on the Schoolhouse roof. The author's father, who attended school in the early 1900's noted that snow was an effective means of taking care of a bully. Several of them having had enough, took a young student, dug a hole about two feet deep, had the young student stand in the hole, and then proceeded to pack snow around his feet, thus anchoring him firmly until someone came to his rescue. The corral, to the viewer's right shows one of many such enclosures that formed a large part of the back lots of the town. Glass plate photo by J. W. Towle.

ORDER UPON THE COUNTY SUPERINTENDENT OF PUBLIC SCHOOLS.

No. 1   June 15   1860

The County Superintendent of Public Schools

Of *Mono* County, will draw a Warrant on the County Treasurer, payable out of the *County* School Fund, for

Ninety seven and 50/100 Dollars

In favor of *Rebecca W. Poor* for bearer or Order

on account of *Salary for teaching*

during the present school year, in the *Bridgeport* School District.

N B Hunewill

J. W. Kingsley

John C. Murphey

$97 50/100

School Trustees of *Bridgeport* District.

Mr. Clay Hampton, Bridgeport school teacher. In September of 1886 Hampton married the daughter of Mrs. Diana Fales, Minnie. Photo courtesy Alice Dolan.

moved to Big Pine; W. A. Lindsey, who took over in 1892; and A. W. Berreyessa, who was appointed principal in 1900 and had taught in Lundy before coming to Bridgeport; Miss Winnie Patterson conducted the Primary Department at that time. One of the most involved was Alice Hayes, who had taught the Bridgeport children in 1873; she was elected Mono County Superintendent of Schools in 1874, one of the first women in the State to hold such a position. In 1914 it was reported that she had been assistant to the Superintendent for twenty years.

In early days, attendance was considered to be important enough to the educational process to have an attendance report printed in the local paper; this was done monthly, and in October of 1882, the following was reported, the numbers referring to days present:

187

Geo. Kirkwood 10
E. Kirkwood 20
C. Kirkwood 20
James Kirkwood 20
Bertha Murphey 20
Bobbie Loose 18½
Lewis Murphey 10
Ed Murphey 13
G. Patterson 15
Fred Straub 19
Sam. Summers 20
Ed Wedertz 9
C. Wedertz 10
F. Wedertz 4½
Belle Allen 20

Arthur Allen 20
James Anton 19
Thos. Anton 20
Baxter Barnes 20
Wm. B. Barnes 5
Frank Barnes 15
Marion Barnes 20
Amasa Bryant 19
Garry Clark 19
Charles Day 18
Harvey Day 20
Eddie Gurney 20
Wm. Hughes 20
George Hughes 19½
Frances Hughes 20

The school system included another woman, Mrs. C. W. Sullivan, County Superintendent in 1881.

Another class, circa 1900, assembled on the front steps of the Bridgeport School, Cordelia Hays, standing at rear against door, was then at the helm. Among those pictured are Harvey Ladd, Cord Hayes, both at rear right; the Anderson children, Leavitts, Murpheys, Crawford, Sayre, and little Rowena Wedertz, third from left in the first row. Photo courtesy M. A. Bryant.

188

Notes
From Big Meadows

There was a ball at Bridgeport Friday eve in honor of moving in of the different books of County offices, thereby permanently locating the County Seat there. Fifteen - twenty couples went from Aurora. 3/27/64.

A letter from Bridgeport: It is a lively town; has a restaurant (F. Lobdell) and two fine hotels, a school house, a planing mill, and several business houses. The town is situated on the northeast side of a beautiful valley called Big Meadows. 11/7/77.

About 35 freight teams pass daily over the Big Meadows and Bodie Toll Road. May 1880.

Last Sunday was quite lively in town. All the hay makers were in, and the place was fairly alive with Indians. In the afternoon there were several Indian pony races back on Emigrant Street which attracted something of a crowd. 7/13/81.

Accident—On Sunday last, in Antelope Valley, the mail carrier on that route, in trying to catch his saddle horse, was knocked down and run over by a party on horseback and severely, but not seriously, injured. 12/9/82.

The Stewart residence on Emigrant Street. Note the Church at the viewer's right.
Photo courtesy Grace Crocker.

189

A small residence just west of the old Leavitt-Waltze stables near the corner of Main and Sinclair. The top of the schoolhouse bell can be faintly seen in the upper right edge above the roof.

1,200 head of sheep passed through town. 7/21/83.

W. A. Loose came in from Bodie over Geiger Grade on snowshoes—the trip took five hours. 3/15/84.

Porter gave a dance at Wedertz Hall; the New Year was ushered in by the ringing of the school bell. 1/5/84.

Upper Main Street is flooded; there is a bridge from Sinclair' across to the east at Huntoon's. 4/20/84.

NEW—Bridgeport Livery and Sale Stables—purchased by C. C. Turner and W. P. Brandon from H. L. Leavitt—has large hanging sliding front doors. 1/16/86.

A stone culvert has been put across Main at Sinclair. 5/8/86.

A dance at Wedertz Hall; Prof. Coyle will furnish the music and Mrs. Wedertz the supper. 2/19/87.

Judge Hakes built a barn on the back of his lot from material of Towle's old barn which was on the old Court House lot. Judge Leavitt has a new barn built from materials of the Stanford Hoisting Works at Bodie. 12/17/87.

A snowstorm has left 18 inches and drifts 4-5 feet high. At 7:30 this morning it was 31 degrees below zero. It must have been as low as 36 during the night. A number of sleighs were on the street yesterday—good sleighing will probably continue for 2-3 weeks. 12/31/87.

There is too much yelling and firing of pistols. 8/4/88.

Professor Godfrey made a balloon ascension and parachute decension from the School House Yard. He landed neatly in Day's field. The balloon came down shortly afterward. 11/25/88.

190

Charles M. Stewart at the reins of a heavy sled, the sort used in hauling fire wood, giving children a ride.

It was up to 106° during the week. 8/3/89.

The ditch at the crossing of Main and Sinclair Streets will be diverted to a ditch to be built through Kirkwood Avenue to and across Emigrant Street. This will save the County the expense of continually repairing the bridge at the old crossing. 10/12/89.

A bull fight on Main Street drew a crowd. 11/16/89.

P. Parmeter erected a large building on his lot and north of his residence on School Street to be used for carriage painting. 11/30/89.

Mon., 40 below zero; Tues., 44 below zero; Wed., 40 below; Thurs., 20 below. 1/11/90.

700 lbs. of trout caught on Grant Lake by S. A. Hopkins and N. Huntoon. 11/29/90.

Those who took a sleigh ride to Fales Hot Springs enjoyed music and dancing. 1/30/92.

Ice houses are being stocked with sawdust from Hawks' Mill. 12/4/97 (Ice was cut on the East Walker River and stored in sheds with sawdust as insulation. One such shed burned, leaving standing a massive stack of ice.)

The Main Street of Bridgeport is being paved. 4/25/06.

191

This photo, circa 1898, shows the Odd Fellows and Rebeccas, two of Bridgeport's social organizations, in front of the Courthouse. Seated in the front row from the viewer's left are the following adults: Clara Waltze, Alice Hunewill, A. Hays, Julia Murphey, Lulu Brandon, Flora Wedertz, Nellie Towle, Emma Stewart, Susie Hayes, unknown, May Waltze, Minnie Pimentel, Winnie Patterson, Lily Kirkwood, child Archie Pimentel between the two women, unknown, V. Brown, Mrs. Sinclair, and Mrs. Virden seated at right. In row two are Emma Edmiston, Viola, Minnie Green, Nettie, Charles Hayes, William Hughes; seated just to the left of the Courthouse entrance is William O. Parker, Charles Stewart in center, Patrick Hughes, J. W. Towle, unknown, Joe Brown, Etta Kirkwood, Clara Murphey. Among those standing in the third row are Frank L. Wedertz just left of the Courthouse entrance, Baxter Barnes, Emery Kirkwood, Sam Smith, a bearded Judge Virden, J. D. Murphey, J. M. Sawyer near right window, Bill Adair, George Hughes, Francis Hughes at far right. Photo courtesy Alice Dolan.

A 31½ lb. trout speared in the West Walker River had 5 hooks in its mouth. 6/10/82.

Before dams blocked the spawning routes of the huge cut-throat trout, it was common to find this species in the Big Meadows and in the high lakes connected to the East and West Walker system.

Among the Bridgeport societies were the Good Templars, organized in May of 1878; the Travertine Council, No. 119, of the Chosen Friends; the Odd Fellows' Lodge, No. 386; Alta Lodge No. 333, organized in August of 1897. The Masons were the more lasting of the male lodges, the founding officers being Frank Hunewill, James Goodall, George Fitzpatrick, N. B. Hunewill, Alexander Scott, J. W. Towle, Fred Hardy, Thomas Keables, George Chichester, John F. Parr, and James Hawks. The brick building at the corner of Hays and Main was converted for use of the Masons, the upper floor being remodeled to house the travertine tables and altars.

EARTHQUAKE OF 1872

Bridgeport, April 21, 1872

Dear brother Wilson:

I returned home last night from a trip to Columbus, where I went to sell some butter. I left here on Monday the 8th, from here to Columbus via Aurora is about 130 miles, nearly east, but the road runs considerable out of the course to get there, and is on the other side of the White and Inyo range of mountains, which are crossed at a low pass. I wrote to Edwin a short time before starting and as you was away from home and my time a good deal occupied I thought I would defer writing to you till my return . . . Did you feel anything of the late earthquake? I felt two quite plain ones on the 26th and one on the 11th instant. The one of the 26th caused a good deal of damage in Inyo Co. and a great loss of life near thirty killed a good many more injured. The loss of life was principally or entirely caused by the falling of brick and adobe buildings which buried up the sleeping occupants. I was awakened by it from a sound sleep finding myself rolling from side to side but felt no disagreeable sensation though some at the Bridge felt sick. That of the 11th inst. occurred while I was on the desert between Aurora and Dexters Wells. I had stopped the horses to rest in the sand, and had good opportunity to notice its peculiar features. It was immediately preceded with a singular ringing sound, as if a large circular saw was struck by a mallet while suspended in the air. The shaking lasted for 10 seconds I think. The horses trembled like the ague and it shook me on the seat as if the wagon was running over a rocky road. A small box on the seat beside me was thrown up from the seat several times so I could distinctly hear it dropping on the seat and the bushes and ground seemed moving up and down. No disagreeable feeling except a light numbness in my legs. At Hot Springs (Benton below Adobe Meadows), in the store of Albert Mack formerly of Aurora bottles were thrown from the shelves to the floor . . . buildings strained and creaked like a ship in a storm, but as they were mostly of wood no damage was done, nor was any injury done at Aurora as the shocks were much lighter than further south. Adobe and brick are at a discount in Owens Valley . . . One place (on the way to Columbus) I had to drive 25 miles without water.

Will T. Elliott

The Bridgeport Brass Band, circa 1885. Upper row, viewer's left to right: Will. Hughes, Chas. Day, Will. Butler, Emery Kirkwood, L. A. Murphey, Phil Sheridan, Sam Smith. Lower row, viewer's left to right: Mike Waltze, Oscar R. Brown, Joe A. Brown, Charles Hayes. Oscar and Joe Brown kept a store on the north side of Main Street opposite the Leavitt House. After the fire of 1908, F. L. Wedertz and Brown flipped a coin to see who would remain in business, Wedertz winning the toss and keeping his newly established general merchandise business.

WALTZE

Located in Big Meadows, roughly opposite Big Hot Springs was the Empire Dairy Ranch of Daniel O. Waltze, who was born in Maine in 1821. He came to California in 1852, located at Chinese Camp, Tuolumne County, and in 1863 moved to Aurora, Nevada. In 1867 Waltze came to Big Meadows and acquired the old Hanson and McCloud ranches, north of that of Wentworth Calkins, and sold dairy products in Aurora. The ranch grew to 1,000 acres before Daniel sold to Kirman and Rickey and left the valley in 1893. Upon his death in 1901, he left two sons, Myron and Alton; and a daughter, Clara. Myron was custodian of the Courthouse for many years; his sleeping quarters were there, and M. A. Bryant recalls that as a boy Myron put him to work, his first job consisting of cleaning all the spittoons. Packing in cord wood from the giant ricks behind the Courthouse was another unpleasant task, but it was pine nut wood that heated the entire

Pioneer of Bodie and Aurora, Mrs. Elizabeth Anne Butler, who was married to Robert Kernohan, Almond Huntoon, and Jesse McGath.

Ben Miller served as Mono County Clerk for three terms. In December of 1887 he married the daughter of A. H. Allen. The handsome brick residence in the north side of upper Main Street is the work of A. J. Severe, who built it for Miller in 1881. In August of that year it was reported that the happy Miller would probably help lay the cornerstone for his new home in Strobridge's saloon. Prior to his public office, he was local agent at Bodie for several fast freight companies.

The DeChambeau Hotel in the early 1900's. The back of the postcard photo reads "Dear Wife: as you have never seen the new hotel thought you may like to know how it looked. So am sending you the picture of it. No news in the town to write you. Landed a bootlegar last night in Masonic. So have got the jail nearly filled up. Has 4 in now, and out after another . . ." Among the Canadians who settled around Mono Lake was six-footer Lewis Winslow DeChambeau. The DeChambeau family gained a reputation as woodsmen and cross country skiers. Descendants of the DeChambeau family remain in Bridgeport Valley. The building shown is the present Bodie Hotel on the corner of Main and School Streets.

building. Myron's wife, Etta, was the daughter of S. M. Booker and the niece of S. G. Cobb, both pioneers of Aurora and Bodie.

Alton, who was the stage driver during the Lundy kidnapping and subsequent shootings involving Wilson and Jardine, operated the old Leavitt Stables on the corner of Main and Sinclair.

195

Camping at Green Creek: from the viewer's left; Mrs. J. W. Towle, young West Smith, Gertrude Towle Smith seated behind her daughter, Naomi, Mrs. F. L. Wedertz, and Frank L. Wedertz.

This photo taken by J. W. Towle can be accurately dated by the following newspaper report of July 29, 1897: "District Attorney J. D. Murphey and family, Deputy Clerk J. W. Towle and wife, and Bert Bernard and family, B. L. Simmons and daughter, Mrs. Joe Beck and daughter Alice, Mrs. Arthur Reading and child, Misses Dell and Lottie Sinnamon, and Winne Patterson are camping at Virginia Creek" when Murphey was struck below the knees by a rolling log. J. W. Towle came to town to get a crutch for him, and, in the photo, Murphey can be seen, crutch under right arm.

196

Helen Anne Kernohan, wife of J. M. Sawyer.

The untimely death of Charles A. Schuman in 1889 at the age of 39 left the family members, Maude and Charles, pictured here. The Schuman residence was on the corner, opposite Bryant's Hall, on Main and School Streets. In 1892 Maude married Charles E. Day of the pioneer G. B. Day family.

Four Bridgeport generations: Standing from the viewer's left are Clara Donnel Murphey and Louisa Wedertz Donnel. Seated is Mrs. L. E. Wedertz. To her right is little Arnot Murphey.

Samuel Hopkins and family. Note Civil War medal.

One of the firm of Anton, Hopkins, and Caine, builders of the old Mono County Courthouse, was Sammuel A. Hopkins, who learned his trade at the shipyard of H. M. Bean at Camden, Maine. Born at Camden in 1834, Hopkins served through the Civil War in a Maine regiment and afterwards came to California. He arrived in Bridgeport in time to assist in the 1877 construction of the Leavitt House. A daughter of the Hopkins-Leavitt marriage became the wife of Frank Waltze. Aside from the fine craftsmanship Hopkins brought to Bridgeport from the Maine shipyard and used in the building of the Courthouse, much of the joinery and detail work of the latter being Hopkins', he built boats for recreational use on Twin, Grant, and Lundy Lakes. The accompanying photograph shows Hopkins, standing at the viewer's left, in front of his home which he built on the southeast corner of Main and Sinclair. The third to the left of Hopkins is W. O. Parker, then John Merrick Sawyer, and Alton Waltze, the last man remaining unidentified, the second man is Dr. Keables. All were Civil War veterans as the medals denote.

198

Jack Westwood, an old Bodie resident, settled on land between Upper and Lower Twin Lakes in about 1878. In July of 1883, Westwood, who was a fisherman and supplied Bridgeport and Bodie with fish had a dispute with a Modesto sheepherder over sheep grazing on Westwood's grass and garden. Westwood settled it with his double barreled shotgun, shooting and killing the sheepherder. Westwood, a Civil War Veteran, as can be noted in the photograph showing him wearing a medal, had a witness who helped in his defense. Westwood was acquitted, and a Modesto newspaper shot back: "Some of the officers of Mono County are the most corrupt and worthless in California." The judge, they claimed, was drunk. Westwood, a native of Wales, stayed on at his home between the lakes until his death in 1907. In addition to the sheepherder incident, Westwood apparently became the first game warden of Mono County.

These four young men are, standing from the reader's left, Clarence Wedertz, Bill Butler; seated from left, Will. Cargill and Baxter Barnes. Clarence attended the School of Mines at the University of Nevada, worked at the Dunderberg mine during some of his schooling, kept a meat market at Bodie, followed the rush to Tonopah, Goldfield, Bullfrog, and Rhyolite, Nevada, tried again to strike it rich and returned to prospect near Bridgeport at Masonic, and eventually settled for the Office of Mono County Weights and Measures. Bill Butler, son of Aurora and Bodie pioneer, Wilson Butler, was a teamster. Will. Cargill took up land at the end of upper Twin Lake, where, in the 1890's, he and his wife Dora Wedertz homesteaded the then remote land now known as Mono Village. Baxter Barnes represents an old family of Big Meadows headed by James Barnes, who left the valley in 1885 to help his sons settle in Modoc County. While Mono residents Reason, William, Andrew, and James both ranched and were teamsters and builders.

The Thomas Kirkwood family originated in New Brunswick, Thomas being an early Big Meadows arrival. In 1871 he purchased the 440 acre Bradley ranch. George and Stewart carried on in ranching and in 1901 purchased the old Sinnamon Dairy where they had been producing gilt butter. George, pictured here, married the daughter of A. L. Butterfield, the Lundy Postmaster, in 1899. He served as Sheriff of Mono County. In 1896, Charles purchased the old Waltze ranch house and had it moved to the northwest corner of Kirkwood Lane, a home for his new wife, Pearl.

Clarence Wedertz standing by truck loaded with quarried travertine. Photo taken in front of F. L. Wedertz Store.

The Travertine Deposit

In the mid 1890's Bridgeport looked with optimism to the newly discovered travertine deposit, a form of banded aragonite, found in a series of enlarged and raised moles about ½ mile southeast of the town. W. E. Lindsey, of Antelope Valley, was the discoverer and developer, although San Francisco partners were instrumental in the development of the deposit.

In September of 1895, a boarding house had been erected at the deposit, a blacksmith shop was added; and on June 27, 1896, the whistle at the quarry blew for the first time. As part of his promotion, Lindsey had, in 1893, shipped seven tons of travertine to the Mid Winter Fair at San Francisco. One of the blocks weighed about five tons, and its beautiful banded colors attracted the attention of many architects and capitalists.

When the company began quarrying operations, E. P. Gray of San Francisco was President, and Joe A. Brown of Bridgeport was Superintendent. Orders were on hand for the Call and Parrott buildings in San Francisco, and slabs decorated the Bridgeport Odd Fellows Hall where the Travertine Council conducted its secret ceremonies. One of the local bars was named the Travertine.

Specimens were taken to New York; there was agreement that the Bridgeport travertine was finer than that of Italy or France, the only other known deposits. Soon the vestibule of the San Francisco Mills Building was wainscoted, and the Crocker Bank and the Palace Hotel showed fine specimens. The lower rotunda of the dome of San Francisco's City Hall was wainscoted with

201

Bridgeport travertine, and, until the disaster of 1906, it was the finest display of colored marble in the United States.

Although the deposit appeared to be extensive, most of the six moles (they were up to fifteen hundred feet long and twenty-five feet high) were composed of white porous limestone, very calcareous and not suitable for polishing. The moles appear to have been formed as hot mineral-charged water rose to the surface in springs and deposited iron, magnesite, aragonite, and other minerals as a result of cooling. The cooling resulting in the precipitation of the minerals. The hot water ran down hill, forming the six almost parallel moles.

Several moles are in the process of formation, and the deposit is an interesting geological curiosity. At the end of one of the moles is an old wooden bath tub, now shrunken in volume by a heavy coating of travertine. While taking a bath, the bather allowed the tub to fill and then diverted the hot water down the center of the mole and waited while the tub water cooled.

The deposit was a favorite camping spot for Indians, and remains of their presence are evident. The hot water was of great value during winter months, and the area probably had ceremonial significance for them. In 1894, human bones were found in a deep cavity, and the workers were told by an old Indian that long ago when deep snow threatened the Indians there with starvation, a man and a woman were killed so that the rest could eat and survive.

Later
Placer
Mining

The water rights suit between Kirman and Rickey and N. B. Hunewill involved a third party who lost both money and water, the Virginia Creek Hydraulic Mining Association. Fortunately for the mining company much of its placer ground lay along Mill Creek toward Mono Lake so additional water was available. The placer mining company had been formed on June 24, 1882, by N. H. N. Brown, John I. Ginn, J. C. Kemp, Edward Manton, William L. Callahan, and Andrew Barnes. D. E. Jones had also been one of the locators and organizers. At this time they had 160 acres of gravel banks and 10,000 inches of water.

The property was reorganized and became the Mono Lake Hydraulic Mining Company. In 1888 the property had grown to over 3,000 acres of placer ground, the pay dirt being irregularly distributed over areas varying greatly in width. The gravel deposits were mined by cuts driven in at bedrock level by hydraulic monitors, the gravel being then run through sluices to collect the gold. At this time the company employed twelve men. The pipe men received four dollars per day each; the others each received $3.50. Mining operations were carried on only for seven months of the year, because of extreme cold, and the gold production from 1883 to 1888 was estimated at $50,000.[1]

By 1889 the Mono Lake Hydraulic Mining Company had been busily floating shares on the London and San Francisco stock markets. That same year the company was involved in litigation, and in 1897 more litigation resulted in the sale of the property at Sheriff's Sale. Included in the sale was the one story R. N. Graves Lodging House and the Office building, located along Mill Creek in Section 13. The small town of Vernon, named for one of the placer claims, was abandoned about this time; a small cemetery remains near the base of Copper Mountain.

1. *Report of the State Mineralogist,* 1888.

The Brick
Ah Quong Tia and Indians

"The Brick" was owned by A. J. Severe, a Bridgeport rancher who, in 1886, owned the two-story brick saloon building as well as a 160 acre ranch complete with house. The actual construction of the Severe brick building may have occurred in the fall of 1880 when it was reported that James Byrnes was going to erect a two-story brick building near the Courthouse. In early days the building was bounded on the west by the Donnel house and on the east by the residence of D. C. Simpson.

In the photo of The Brick, taken by Towle in about 1896, "The Brick", one of the most popular saloon locations, was bounded on the west by the Courthouse Corner Saloon, and on the east by the Travertine Saloon. At this time "The Brick" was operated by F. M. "Pike" Richardson, who had left Boone County, Missouri, on May 2, 1849, crossed the plains and arrived in California August 2, 1849. "Pike" was one of the earliest of Bridgeport farmers. In 1899, a brother, Jesse Green Richardson, died, having lived in Mono County twenty years.

O. F. Strobridge kept a saloon in the building in 1880 and put down the old boardwalk. Tom Fales took over and operated the Palace Saloon there until 1894 when he sold to "Pike", who had been a mixologist in partnership with C. B. Anton further east on Main Street. Then, in 1897, J. M. Sawyer moved his saloon business at the Courthouse Corner into "The Brick".

It seemed a Western practice to use the second floor of saloons as a justice court, so the second floor of the old brick, because of its close proximity to the Courthouse, was used as justice court;

204

The store building occupied by Ah Quong Tia. Being roped and dragged the length of Main Street and then butchered obviously put an end to his occupancy here. The building was located near the present Sturgeon home on Court Street; to the rear can be seen the small Pedrocini cabin where miner Ed. Page often wintered. What has long been known as the Coasting Hill forms the horizon, the latter being a spot for winter sledding. Photo courtesy M. A. Bryant.

it was here that the trial of Ah Quong Tia took place, an event that turned the town into an armed camp.

After much of the old town had been abandoned in favor of sites around the new Court House, several Chinese moved into old buildings left vacant east of the river on Court Street. There Ah Quong Tia ran a small store on the south side of the street and dealt in general Indian trade, gambling, whisky, and opium. Quite suddenly Bridgeport found itself surrounded by Indians from Bodie, Mono Lake, and the Walker Lake Reservation, Indians who were in search of Poker Tom. The Reservation Indians, seventy-five well armed and drilled men, were led by Captain Charley. Sheriff Cody and concerned citizens quickly met with them to help in the search.

Tom was known to have visited Bridgeport in mid-April. He got into a poker game with some Chinese and left a fifty dollar winner. He then bought some calico at Bryant's Store and supposedly headed for the Walker River Reservation.

Captain Charley's delegation, in company with Sheriff Cody, searched the store of Quong Tia, where Indians had noticed blood spots on the floor boards, the store in which Poker Tom was last seen by some. Although the floor boards had been repeatedly washed by Tia, the keen-eyed Indians had them pulled up; much more blood was visible. Now it became known that the Indians had arrived with much more than suspicions in regard to Tia; the horrible discovery of a human torso in the Walker River had led them to Tia.

Tia was quickly arrested and charged with the crime of killing, dismembering, and throwing the remains of Tom into the

205

river in Bryant's field. He had tried to leave town the night of the murder but did not succeed in disposing of his goods, which he tried to sell to Hays.

Court was quickly called into session on the second floor of the Severe "Brick". Tia had engaged John C. Murphey and W. O. Parker to defend him, and at ten o'clock in the morning Tia's examination before Justice Thomas Fales began. The prisoner entered in charge of Deputy Constable Crowell. Deputy District Attorney Hayes represented the people. The examination was held behind closed doors, but when the prisoner was taken upstairs, the Indians posted themselves at the rear of the building to prevent Tia from being taken away through the rear windows. A large number of Indians guarded the front, some having horses ready in case pursuit would be necessary. There were squads all along lower Main Street and a large reserve near the bridge, with horses ready in case the whites attempted to shield Tia.

During the testimony of County Physician Dr. T. A. Keebles, it was noted that the cutting had been done with a keen knife and a fine toothed saw. The remarkably preserved remains of what appeared to be Poker Tom had been covered with a solution of chloride of lime and ammonia. All that could be determined was that it was the body of an adult.

The Indians, however, were certain Tia had murdered Tom and expected no interference from the whites since they, the Indians, had turned over to the whites the murderer of Louis Samman. Tia was discharged; against his pleadings for protection, he was released. The Indians quickly took him from in front of "The Brick", rushed up Main Street to Day's field and quickly executed and dismembered Tia. The remains were left exposed, and the Indians returned quietly to their camp. Later, at the request of Dr. Keebles, Captain John took a few Indians and had the various remains gathered in a blanket and buried in Sinnamon's field.

In contrast to the dismissal of Tia, Frank Hanson and M. P. Hayes testified that Tia had confessed to the killing, that Tom had won $54 from Tia, who then wanted his money back. They fought, Tia eventually clubbing Tom to death and dismembering the body.

One fact was certain: the entire town was helpless before the Indian forces that suddenly had appeared. Families of whites were hurried to hotels for safety, Sheriff Cody sending his family to the Leavitt House. A posse of armed veterans was stationed around the Courthouse to protect that building and the jail. There were rumors that some Indians had threatened to burn the town if Tia were not released to them. Large fires were kept burning in the hills east of town. Sheriff Cody and others had met directly with the Indians and had pacified them while the trial was in progress.

Some of the townspeople even blamed the State Government for the unfortunate affair, pointing out that for the past twenty years Mono had repeatedly requested that a company of the National Guard be allotted due to the remote location of the County.

The Grand Jury, however, found that Tia was the murderer of Tom and that the Superior Court had not received incriminating evidence from the Coroner's Jury. It also felt that the Justice erred in discharging Tia from custody, that the lack of an objection to the dismissal by the Deputy District Attorney was an error, and that the defending attorneys erred in releasing Tia against his own requests. The Grand Jury felt that the Sheriff should have protected Tia from what was felt to be certain death at the hands of the Indians and censured the Sheriff for that as well as his having made no attempt to arrest the murderers of Tia.[1]

Others felt that the town had been ridded of a scoundrel and that the Sheriff did well in not pursuing a course that would have led to further bloodshed. Perhaps the most succinct statement of the entire affair was made by an Indian witness who testified at the Grand Jury hearing as follows:: "Our Chief say no talk; Tom dead, Tia dead; pretty good."[2] And, an advertisement of Tia's, which was printed four years before his death, closed with the following ironic request: "Kindly give me a trial".[3] At that time he had been operating a laundry near the old Allen House Hotel.

The accompanying photos show two Indian women with children, one especially handsomely dressed by white standards. In the mid 1880's, the Indian population of Mono was estimated at about five hundred. In 1891, the population was reported to be 375, Bridgeport and Homer Townships accounting for 83. The pine nut was the main food supply; in the late fall the Indians crossed the Sierra to Tuolumne and gathered acorns and traded goods such as obsidian, pine nuts, and salt. The Piutes and Monos, a branch of the latter, held large gatherings at the northeast shore of Mono Lake and at Coleville where feasting and

1. *Bridgeport Chronicle-Union,* 12/5/91.
2. Ibid., 12/5/91;   6/13/91.
3. Ibid., 12/24/87.

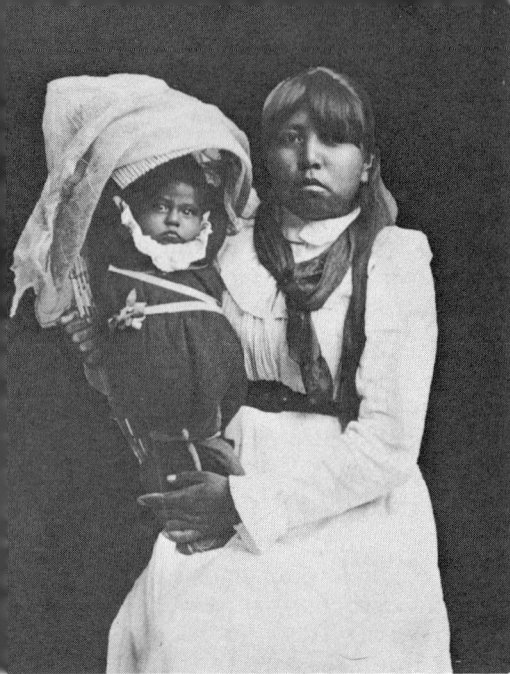

games took place. Hundreds of Indians were attracted to these events. In 1884 some five hundred gathered at Coleville. In August of 1881, a large group of Monos was reportedly harvesting the larvae at Mono Lake, the food for which they were named.

Bridgeport has been the site of an Indian colony for many years, old pictures show Indian structures east of the river. Unfortunately, the only news usually reported in local papers concerned itself with whisky and violence. There was little mention of Indian culture and values since they differed so widely from that of most whites. One Bodie item refers to the playing of an Indian ball game, keema-a-nut-a-wee, on the ice of the Standard Mining Co. pond. Foot-racing and gambling games were rarely mentioned, the crafts of arrowhead and basket making were seemingly ignored until recently. One of the most strict of county ordinances was passed at the request of John Sides, the Piute officer from the Walker Lake Reservation; this 1889 ordinance made it a misdemeanor for Indians to be on the streets between sunset and sunrise. Apparently Sides was attempting to protect his people from white habits.

208

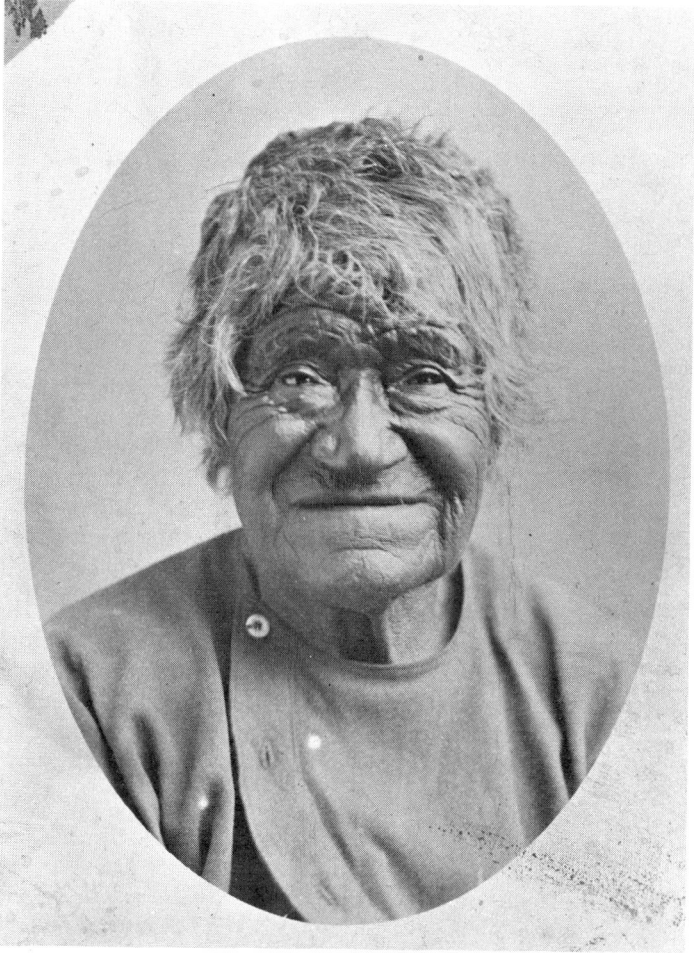

Captain Jim, shown in the accompanying photo, was an early chief. Jack Lundy was a chief who was very popular among both whites and Indians. In 1860, Wazadazzobabahago, head medicine man of the Monos amazed Indian Agent Warren Wasson with a fantastic ritual of resurection, and Wasson said that if he had not seen it himself he would not have believed it. Over 1,500 Indians had assembled at the mouth of Walker River and war was threatened; Bannocks from Oregon and Idaho aided the Pah-utes, but peace was established. Bridgeport seemed to have escaped the Pyramid Lake and Owens Valley out right wars, but the settlement of the Big Meadows was not without confrontations. The Ah Quong Tia affair resulted in a frightening show of strength by Indian forces.

Bridgeport Fires

In 1893 a fire house was constructed between the barber shop and Kirkwood's saloon on the north side of Main Street. Judge Virden, C. L. Hayes, A. C. Folger, B. L. Simmons, and J. D. Murphey had met and organized a hook and ladder company. The small fire house covered a two-wheeled hook and ladder truck, which had been purchased for $278. As was the case in most early camps and towns the venture proved to be an exercise in futility.

In December of 1888, the third fire had struck. The first occurred in 1881, the second fire was the burning of the jail by Ye Park in 1883. This third one destroyed three Chinese houses in back of the Whitman building east of the river and on the south side of Court Street. These three fires were nothing in comparison to what broke out at 11:30 p.m. on the 5th of May, 1908, the greatest fire in the history of Bridgeport Valley.

On that night of May 5th, someone set fire to Simmons' Building; he oiled a wall and lit a match. A gale was blowing; B. L. Simmons, asleep upstairs, heard the flames. The fire and the wind was too much, and very quickly the fire burned out the Simmons Building, spread east along the north side of Main Street and quickly destroyed Brown's Store, the D. M. Walters Saloon, the unoccupied McGath residence, Bryant's barn, and, ironically, the fire house.

Heroic work by the volunteer firefighters was exhausting. Suddenly, the wind changed; this saved the town. The Leavitt House, Bryant's Store, and the Smith House were all in danger; the heat was so great that paint bubbled and woodwork charred within ten minutes after the first alarm. Then buildings were in ruins, sparks and coals had spread quickly during the heavy wind. The loss was set at $19,000, the low figure indicating the economic depression that gripped Bridgeport after the collapse of Bodie and held the County until recently when tourism and recreation brought the County to life.

210

Ludowig Edmund Wedertz; photo taken at Amsterdam circa 1872.

Mrs. L. E. Wedertz with son, Frank L., the latter born at the Friedell ranch on the East Walker River in 1876. In 1900 Frank bought out Stewart Kirkwood to become sole proprietor of the Bridgeport Market. In February of 1926 he sold the store to Cain and Evans and then became Tax Collector.

Wedertz

The accompanying photograph shows Ludowig (Louis) Edmund Wedertz, born in 1824 at Arensburg, Germany. His departure from Germany was rather unusual in that he, with the help of friends, stowed himself in a crate that was later placed on board a ship. In the process the crate was dropped in the sea but was quickly recovered. The plan allowed Wedertz to avoid serving in the wars between the German States.

He arrived at New Orleans about 1845, married Niklamine Maria Dorthea Wischmann there in 1851. They decided to strike out for California, crossing Panama by foot with mules as pack animals. Accompanying them was their infant daughter, Louisa. The three arrived in San Francisco about September of 1853.

L. E. Wedertz, as he was commonly known, was the thirteenth child and the eleventh son of a family of fifteen. Apparently large families were comfortable for him, he and his wife eventually having eleven children, eight of which survived and later settled in Bridgeport and Smith valleys.

211

Dora Wedertz in an early photo taken at Hannover. Dora was first married to Washington P. Brandon and they had three children. She later married William Cargill.

A photo of Bertha Wedertz Logan, taken by J. C. Kemp of Bodie. Bertha was born in San Francisco in 1860 just before the family moved to Sulphur Springs.

Two men on horseback on the west side of the old L. E. Wedertz Store building. To the viewer's left can be seen the bridge crossing; the Brandon ranch house is beyond the bridge. Photo by Towle circa 1898.

L. E. Wedertz entered the merchandise and grocery business and kept stores on Tehama and Kearny Streets until about 1862 when the family followed the rush to Aurora and opened a stage station at Sulphur Springs on the Carson-Aurora road. They remained there until about 1866 when they moved to Aurora; after two years there they returned to Sulphur Springs. In 1869 they began a trip that took them to Iowa, where a branch of the Wedertz family had settled and engaged in merchandising, then on to Germany to return, by 1874, to America at the old Friedell ranch just south of Bridgeport on the East Walker River. There Clarence R. and Frank Lewis were born, the latter in 1876. Charles Edward had been born at Sulphur Springs in 1865. A first-born son, Lewis, had died in infancy and was buried on the hill east of the old station. Another son, born in Iowa, died when the family was in Germany.

213

A photo from a glass plate made by Towle and captioned "House Moving: Clarence Wedertz, having purchased a lot on Emigrant Street near the head of School Street and just northwest of the CHRONICLE-UNION Office, is now having the large two-story Wedertz building hauled from the foot of Main Street to the new lot." 1/19/01, BRIDGEPORT CHRONICLE-UNION. The building shown is the old store of L. E. Wedertz built in 1881. The amazing Washington P. Brandon is using his team to move the building, which is sliding on skids over the snow. Indian cabins at the site of the present Indian Colony can be seen in the distance. The old store building is now used as a church at its present location on Emigrant Street.

The interior of the F. L. Wedertz Store shows, at the viewer's left, Mrs. Lyna May Sawyer Wedertz and her son, Gilbert, J. M. Sawyer, and Frank L. Wedertz. Frank L. had married Lyna May Sawyer in 1899; Gilbert was born in 1904.

At this time L. E. Wedertz was planning a store in Bridgeport and had five hundred feet of 16-foot boards stacked at the old bridge. It was 1875; the lumber was from the Eagle Sawmill, but it was not until May of 1881 that it was reported that carpenters Foley and Lynch were erecting a large two-story building, 34 x 14 feet. The first floor was to be used as a store, the second as a public hall. The building was erected immediately east of the Towle residence on the south side of Bridge Street and was attached to the front of the old Nye Mill near the East Walker River. His competition was Hays, Brown, and Bryant. On the same day, the local news included the following:

> *"Independent—Yesterday the Wedertz and Donnel families went to the West Walker on a picnic excursion, to be gone several days—until the 'staff of life' gives out . . . New Goods—Reason Barnes' mountain clippers arrived here on Thursday from Carson with new goods for Hays Bros., and L. E. Wedertz. Give them a call."* 7/16/81, Bridgeport Chronicle-Union.

Suddenly, as the result of a rib piercing a lung, L. E. Wedertz was dead. It was December of 1881. His widow carried on the merchandise business for several years; and their children, some already married, soon populated the town. The five daughters, Louisa, Emma, Dorothea, Adelia, and Bertha all married established Bridgeport businessmen.

215

The interior of the F. L. Wedertz Store. From the viewer's left are Robert Sawyer, Washington P. Brandon, Emmett Hayes, and Frank L. Wedertz. Photo circa 1910.

In this photo of the Frank L. Wedertz Store and Butcher Shop, old bamboo fishing poles may be seen above the Prince Albert Tobacco sign. From the viewer's left are Emmett Hayes, Washington P. Brandon, Frank L. Wedertz, Dave LeRoy, M. A. Bryant, and Robert W. Sawyer seated in the Ford. The Ford was used for deliveries; peeking out of the back window is Louie Sam. The old saloon building, to the viewer's right, was used as a storehouse and later became part of the Wedertz store. Together the buildings form the center of the present Bridgeport General Store. The central building, also formerly used as a saloon, may be what old timers called the Gurney Building.

Scene taken at Jordon showing the wreckage caused by the storm of 1911.

The Storm of 1911

In June of 1960 Steven Scanavino, who was raised at the old Scanavino Ranch near Mono Lake, wrote a lengthy article in which he recalled the events and the effects of the storm of 1911 when a massive snow slide slipped off the entire east side of Copper Mountain and absolutely destroyed the power plant and settlement of Jordan. Seven men died in the Jordan slide, and a woman who had been buried deep under the snow was rescued after having suffered for over sixty hours in her tomb-like enclosure. This was one of several such disasters that occurred between March 7 and March 18th.

Scanavino, one of the Jordan rescue party, recalled that it began snowing in December of 1910, and snowed heavily there-

Ice skating has been a popular sport. Here Frank L. Wedertz is pictured as skaters and sleds are captured in the background.

after, the first months of 1911 being a record snowfall. It changed to a wet snow in January, then stopped, and a cold snap froze the surface. Then, in February, snow began to fall heavily and continuously until the disasters of March. It was estimated that the massive slide off Copper Mountain consisted of 4,000,000 tons of snow.[1]

The extent of the storm can be imagined as reports from other parts of the Mono County were collected. A slide at the Golden Gate Mine above Antelope Valley had destroyed the boarding house; other slides there had taken away the bunk house, stable, and an intake at one of the power plants. Fortunately, no men were there at the time. At Silverado Canyon in the Sweetwater Mountains a slide on the 7th carried away the boarding house and stables of the mining company. A fortunate boarder living in the assay office was not caught by the slide, but snow covered up the building, only the chimney sticking out. What could be termed a huge snowball came down the mountainside at Mono Lake and crowded the postoffice building into the lake. In the deep canyon where Lundy is located two slides hit, and the entire population of Lundy was gathered in the hotel there, which was considered the safest place. From Masonic came dreadful news, Samuel M. Smith had been killed in a snowslide about three miles from the camp.

1. *Mineral County Independent News*, 2/26/62.

Winter at Masonic Gulch.

Masonic Mining District

In the summer of 1860, prospectors from Monoville discovered promising leads around what is now called Masonic Mountain. News from July of that summer reported rich leads. The discoverers, being Masons, labeled the new district Masonic. An old Monoville resident, Jacob Rodenbaugh, recalled that two men from Illinois, Atcheson and Alberton, were among the discoverers. The rich Aurora strike of August of 1860 captured the attention of all, and it was not until forty years later that the Masonic mines were re-discovered and Bridgeport and the County looked forward to a mining excitement that all hoped would equal that of the Bodie boom.

John S. Phillips, Caleb Dorsey, and John M. Bryan made the re-discovery on July 4, 1902 at what was to become the Pittsburg-Liberty Mine, located off the north slope of Masonic Mountain. It was 1904 before the property was developed by shafts and tunnels blocking out the ore bodies for extraction. The gold occurred in a porphry dike running north and south between granite, and assays ran from $35 to $800 per ton. The vein was from three to twelve feet in width and highgrade ore at $1,500 per ton was struck in quantity enough to sack and ship out for special treatment.

219

M. P. Hayes standing at the door of his tent cabin at Masonic. Photo courtesy Alice Dolan. Photo circa, 1905.

When C. R. Wedertz arrived at the Masonic Gold Excitement in January of 1904 he noted that about twenty men were at the camp in Masonic Gulch, and they promptly re-organized the district and drew up by-laws. About ten claims were being worked, and echoes from the blasting rocked across the hills about the gulch. Doctor Krebs, Dan Smith, and Frank Waltze were all busily locating and working ground. Rich strikes in the Pittsburg-Liberty motivated them all to continue to prospect and mine what were to become, for most, unproductive sites. In November of 1904 Phillips added to the excitement by displaying a piece of highgrade gold, which assayed at $4,000 a ton, from a claim he bought for $49. But the future was not all riches for Phillips; in July of 1909 he was killed in the Pittsburg-Liberty Mine as the result of a 160 foot fall down a raise. He had, however, witnessed a curiosity that added to his wealth before his death. In 1905 it was discovered that the Pittsburg-Liberty had been using, as a wall for one of its tunnels, the side of a vein that proved to be one of their main ledges. The ledge was over two feet wide and assayed over $200 per ton.

Roads were quickly pushed through to Masonic from Bridgeport and Bodie. In the summer of 1904, the first cabin was built

220

Masonic - Mill
1916

ILL-BROS.
MILL
SONIC, CAL.
JAN, 1916.

Two views of the Stall Brothers Mill at Lower Town. Note the cabin at the right. The mill was run by electricity generated from a point on the East Walker River below the old Conway Ranch and near the bridge across the river on the road to Bodie and Aurora. This was also known as the Pittsburg-Liberty Mill as the mill included a cable and bucket system which ran across the gulch to the west to the Pittsburg-Liberty works. Ore was also delivered by wagon via the road behind and in front of the Mill.

221

A more recent photo of those who continued on in hopes of another strike. Seated at the viewer's left is Dan M. Smith, original locator of the Pittsburg Extension and son-in-law of J. W. Towle. Standing at the left edge of the ore car and wearing the darker hat is C. R. Wedertz. To the extreme right is Gilbert Wedertz.

at what was to become part of the town of Masonic, located in Masonic Gulch. The cabin, 18 x 20 feet, was made of aspen logs, had a floor of one-inch boards, and displayed a glass paneled door for class. This was the residence of Mr. and Mrs. H. Carpenter, and was located in Middle Town Masonic. The cabin was part of the property of the Myrtle and Julia Mining Company of which George Montrose, Carpenter, J. M. Sawyer, Dr. Krebs, John Saxe, H. H. Boone, and Geo. Vansickle were interested. A fifty foot shaft was sunk on the property and four hundred feet of tunneling was done. The production was apparently discouraging, but not for George Montrose who had taken over the old *Bridgeport Chronicle-Union*. On November 8, 1905, he issued the first number of what was to become the short-lived *Masonic Pioneer* newspaper. Quite a crowd gathered at the first printing to tap a keg of beer.

222

This glass plate photo by J. W. Towle shows Lower Town before the Stall Bro. Mill was constructed; the construction of the mill eliminated the two cabins to the viewer's left. The cabin at the right, below the large outcropping remained. Eventually, a road between Lower Town and the East Walker River, to the north, was built and left Lower Town via the saddle in the ridge. This portion of Masonic was also known as Calaveda, or Caliveda. All three cabins are on the east side of the Gulch.

Another view of Lower Town looking southeast up Masonic Gulch toward Middle Town. The structures were obviously not built in the hopes of developing a lasting town.

A. J. W. Towle photo showing Lorena, or Upper Town. Here was located the post office, the offices of the Pittsburg-Liberty and the Masonic Mountain Gold Mining Company. The photo shows a little of the Pittsburg-Liberty hill, to the viewer's right. At the head of the photo is the cabin of J. M. Sawyer. Photo taken in 1904.

The Gulch was now the site of a small camp, and buildings strung along its course soon constituted the Upper, Lower, and Middle towns of Masonic. Lower Town was at the north, almost opposite the Pittsburg-Liberty Mine. In Middle Town, on the east side of the Gulch, was the other major mine, the Jump-Up-Joe. The name of the mine may have had something to do with the fact that the mine follows a huge dike in which free gold was found in boulders on the surface. This property was involved in some litigation since it was located by a miner named Green and sold by the young man for a small sum. The sale was not contested until rich ore was found.

In Middle Town was the H. Boone & Son Store and the ill-fated printing office of the *Masonic Pioneer*. The first child born at Masonic was a girl, the parents being Mr. and Mrs. Joseph K. Weitfle, the date was September 29, 1905. Weitfle and Slim Eastwood were interested in another of the Masonic mines, the True Friend, which was part of the property of the Masonic Mountain Gold Mining Company. Others involved in the new camp of Masonic included F. L. Wedertz, who opened a butcher shop.

Mining property that was being worked included the Sarita, the New York, the South End, Red Rock, Anaconda, and Gold Bug. Masonic Mountain, formed of granite and schists, was traversed at the north and east edges by dikes; the better claims occurred in this formation, but only the Pittsburgh-Liberty and the Jump-Up-Joe were reputed to have been bullion producers and the camp soon folded.

In 1909 C. R. Wedertz noted that the True Friend Mine alone employed nine men and ran three shifts. In August of 1911 he reported that there was only one man, the postmaster, in Middle Town and no one in Upper Town.[1] "The Camp has never been this deserted," he wrote.

1. Frickstad: A post office was established at Lorena on 12/6/05.

MORE Notes
FROM Big MeadoWS

"Every other man in Bridgeport is a lawyer and the next fellow keeps a saloon." 3/15/82, *Bodie Weekly Standard-News.*
"A big team—Frank Doten passed through town, on Sunday, en route for Carson. The team of 16 horses were hitched to 5 wagons." 12/24/87, *Bridgeport Chronicle-Union.*

"Dangerous—Now that the baseball club has reorganized we suggest that it find a better place than Main Street for ball playing. The last time they played told them plainly it was no good to have such sport in town, as they are liable to break every window glass within range. Their last game resulted in breaking the heavy plate glass in the window of the Sheriff's Office, and the running into of County Clerk Murphey, knocking him down and injuring his knee, which confined him to his house several days and necessitating the use of crutches. It is not generally known that the Penal Code makes it a misdemeanor to use the streets of a city or town for horse racing, ball playing . . ." 4/6/95 *Bridgeport Chronicle-Union.*

"Wood Traffic—Our wood dealers are making the most of the present fine weather to fill their wood contracts, and wood piles are growing to goodly portions all over town. The Piutes will find no scarcity of work this winter for 'hogadie'—wood teams can be seen at all hours of the day passing through our streets loaded with this indispensible article of domestic use, and Emery E. Kirkwood and James Logan have ornamented the *Chronicle-Union* lot with thirteen cords of nutpine with which we hope to thwart the inroads Jack Frost may attempt between now and next April. When we see twenty cords of County wood corded up back of the Court House, and handy to our own office, we shall feel still more safe from visits from the Frost King." 11/23/95, *Bridgeport Chronicle-Union.*

"The Ice Harvest—Our citizens who have ice houses are making preparations for putting in their ice crop at the proper time, when the mercury runs down into the 20's below zero, as they are gathering loads of sawdust for its preservation. Alex F. Scott brought in a big load on Tuesday from Hawk's sawmill. It is not likely there

227

The log cribbed dam which was built in the 1890's by the Standard Con. Mining Co. of Bodie formed what is known as Dynamo Pond on Green Creek. It was built under the supervision of millwright Andrew Smith to provide water storage and water power to generate electricity in the Dynamo below.

will be any difficulty in gathering all the ice required for next summer's use." 12/4/97, *Bridgeport Chronicle-Union.*

"Whisky Famine—Bridgeport has been undergoing a whisky famine, but it was broken on Thursday evening when Thos. Raycroft brought in on the Carson Stage a barrel of whisky for the Wolverine Saloon. Such a famine is a terrible thing for this town, but we believe it is the first time such a deplorable affair has happened, and it is safe to say it will never be repeated." (The Wolverine was on the north west corner of Main and Sinclair).

"C. M. Stewart has been busy hauling ice—two feet thick—from Dynamo pond for B. L. Simmons who proposes to keep his customers cool this summer." 2/3/1900, *Bridgeport Chronicle- Union.*

The Dynamo Plant on Green Creek. The line, which ran from the Dynamo to the Standard Con. Mill at Bodie was reputed to be the first long distance hydro-electric transmission in the world. The plant was later used to generate power for the old Silverado Mine, and a line was run there from Green Creek. Photo by J. M. Towle, circa, 1900.

Key to Building Locations

Bridgeport circa 1904, from a photo by Towle. Murven Bryant and Gilbert Wedertz, both born at Bridgeport, helped in the identification of sites shown in the photo. From the mid-1880's until the early 1900's, the town changed very little in structure and residency.

1. Charles Kirkwood home
2. Huntoon residence
3. Hawks residence
4. Maurice Hayes residence
5. Bump residence
6. *Chronicel-Union* Office and Folger residence
7. G. B. Day residence
8. Barn
9. *Chronicle-Union* barn
10. Bryant's barn
11. Hawthorne residence — site of present Memorial Hall
12. Thomas Kirkwood residence
13. Andrew Sayers residence
14. Kirkwood barn
15. Boone barn
16. Huntoon barn
17. Schreck, Smith, Barney Peeler, Ed Wedertz, W. Parker: a group of residences east of the Hawks home.
18. Schoolhouse, s i n c e moved across town to house the present museum.
19. Waltze residence
20. Parmeter residence
21. Virden barn (behind the present Sportsman's Inn restaurant). Simmons barn was on the S.E. corner of Kingsley and Sinclair Streets.
22. Dave Hays barn
23. Murphy barn
24. Brandon residence; at this time was Murphy home.
25. Old Leavitt - Waltze stables, on the northwest corner of Sinclair and Main.
26. The Leavitt House, the present Bridgeport Hotel.
27. A. H. Allen-Brandon Stables
28. D. Hays Store
29. D. Hays warehouse, corner of Main and Hays.
30. Summers residence
31. Ben Miller brick residence
32. Bryant's Hall; site of Slick's Court.
33. Court House, note well-driller's tripod.
34. Simmons Saloon - old Loose building.
35. Bryant's Store
36. A. H. Allen Hotel; between Bryant's store and Allen's were the Bump Market and an old residence occupied at one time by Joseph J. and John N. Dudleston, father and son; both held county offices at the same time.
37. Hughes' Blacksmith S h o p with gallows frame.
38. Stanton Saloon
39. Towle residence
40. L. E.—F. L. Wedertz residence.

41. Old stone jail and attached sheriff's residence.
42. The three numbered locations show the old route of Main Street.
43. Bridge and old crossing of East Walker River.
44. East Walker River

45. Present route of Highway 395.
46. Brandon and Stewart residences.
47. Road south to Bodie and Mono Lake.
48. Buckeye Canyon

Key to Bridgeport Townsite Map

1. Residence built by Jesse Summers, later occupied by J. D. Murphey. Present home of Alice Dolan.
2. Barnes residence.
3. Brick residence of Ben Miller. Next east was the church lot. The foundation for a church was laid but the building was never completed.
4. The Jesse McGath residence; formerly used by Col. Davies.
5. Bryant's Hall.
6. The Court House.
7. The Court House Corner Saloon, 1883.
8. The Brick Saloon built by A. J. Severe.
9. Site of the old Gurney building which later housed the F. L. Wedertz butcher shop and a saloon.
10. The site, now part of the Bridgeport General Store, as is #9, was used as Sinclair's medical office and later as a saloon.
11. The Simmons-Loose saloon building at the site of the present Trails restaurant. It was moved there by Loose from its original site east of the Allen House.
12-13-14-15. These structures composed the following: the fire house, the Kirkwood Saloon, Sparks Barber Shop, Brown's Store, the Crowell residence, the McKinnon or Crowell Building. These housed a variety of tenants and businesses.
16. Bryant's Store and residence.
17. The old Allen House hotel.
18. The old Dudleston home, later occupied by J. J. Welch.
19. Hughes' Blacksmith shop.
20. Sharkey's shoe shop attached to the Stanton Bldg.
21. The Stanton Saloon.
22. Wedertz residence at site of old Nye shingle and planing mill. Site of L. E. Wedertz Store.
23. J. W. Towle residence; the present home of the Huggans.
24. Dave Hays warehouse built in the early 1890's; the upper floor was used for Masons and Odd Fellows.
25. Dave Hays Store and Residence.
26. The grainry, Stables and barn and blacksmith shop of the Allen House, the Allen House, the latter across the street. Later the property of W. P. Brandon.
27. Old residence; possibly the Kingsley-Parrish residence. Ed. Murphy was there. Now the residence of J. Brandon.
28. The P. G. Hughes residence.
29. Doc. Sinclair home. Present residence of Wes Berreyesa. It was also the home of J. M. Sawyer.
30. The Leavitt House; now the Bridgeport Hotel.
31. Residence of Sam. Hopkins.
32. Old Leavitt House Stables; later operated by Waltze.
33. Residence; occupancy unknown.
34. Jefferys home; later the home of Judge Virden. Tradition holds that school was often held here before the school house was built. Site of the present Sportsman's Inn Restaurant.
35. Gurney residence.
36. Eastwood residence.
37. Schuman home site.
38. Delury residence.
39. Residence; occupancy unknown.
40. Residence once occupied by W. O. Parker.

232

41. Andy Sayre residence circa 1906; next door was that of Dr. Atleck.
42. Ada Stewart Boone residence. Site of present Redwood Court.
43. Barn, Hayes.
44. Barn.
45. Simmons Barn.
46. Barn.
47. Parmeter residence.
48. Barn as part of Sinnamon property.
49. Huntoon residence; present Bettancourt home.
50. Barn.
51. Slaughterhouse.
52-53. Barns.
54. Thomas Kirkwood home.
55. Kirkwood residence.
56. Barn.
57. G. B. Day residence.
58. Barn.
59. Cargil Home and Dora Brandon property.
60. Logan residence.
61. Ladd residence.
62. Stewart residence.
63. Church building formerly the store of L. E. Wedertz until moved to this site in 1901.
64. Hawthorne residence; may have been old Donnel home.
65. Barn.
66. Barn.
67. Barn.
68. **Bridgeport Chronicle-Union** Office and residence and barn of the Folgers.
69. Jail and adjoining sheriff's residence.
70. Residence connected to Main street via an alley along the west side of the Court House Corner Saloon. Possibly the Donnel residence.
71. Bryant Barn.
72. Slaughter house at rear of Allen House.
73. M. Hayes residence.
74. Waltze residence.
75. Smith residence.
76. Shed.
77. Schoolhouse; moved to a new site as museum.
78. Parker residence.
79. Barney Peeler cabin.
80. Ed. Wedertz residence.
81. Shreck residence.
82. Smith residence.
83. Hawks residence.
84. Barn.
85. Residence; unknown occupancy.

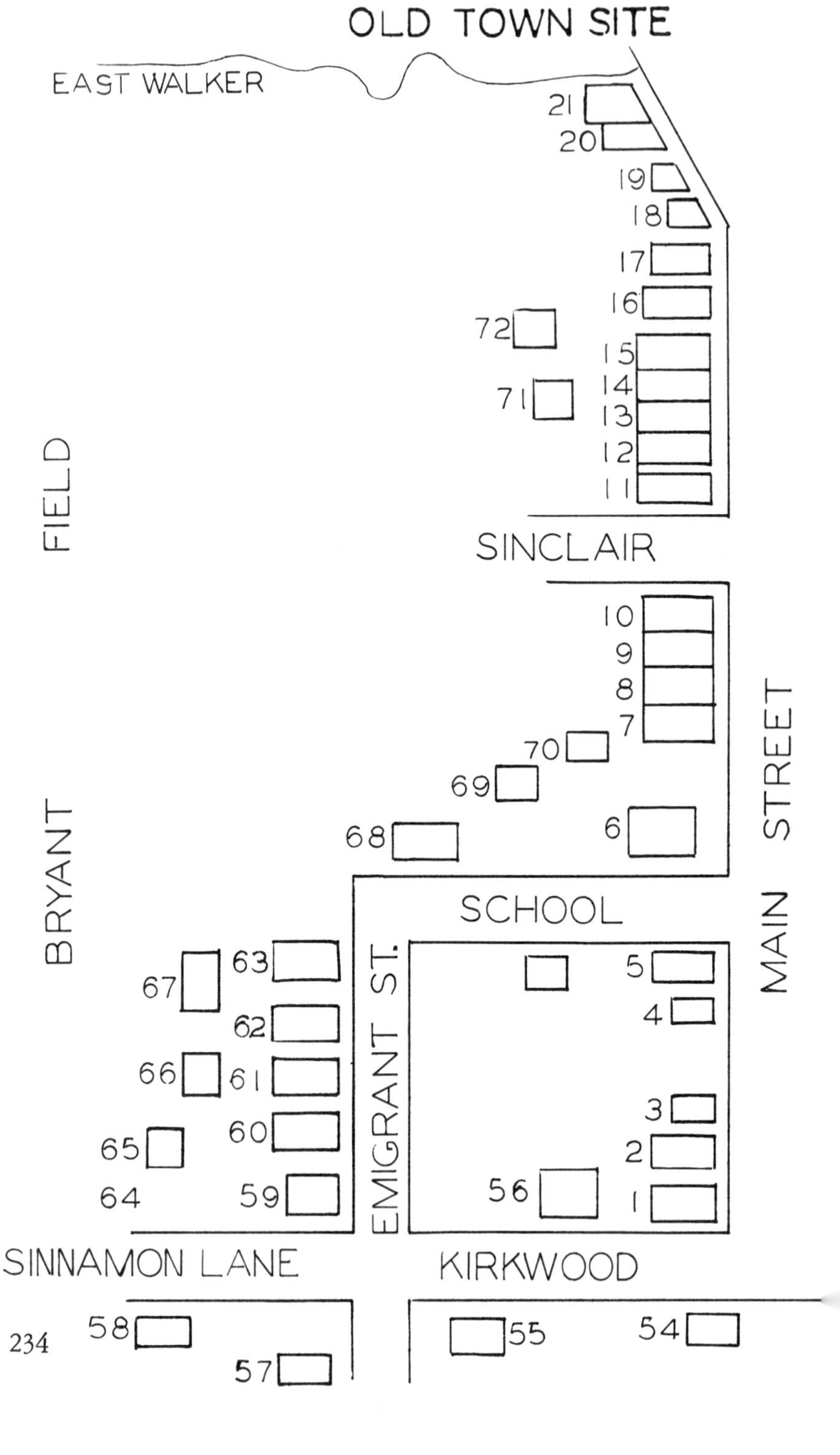

OLD TOWN SITE

EAST WALKER

FIELD

BRYANT

SINCLAIR

MAIN STREET

EMIGRANT ST.

SCHOOL

SINNAMON LANE

KIRKWOOD

234

21
20
19
18
17
16
15
14
13
12
11

72
71

10
9
8
7
70
69
68
6

67 63
62
66 61
60
65
64 59

5
4
3
2
56 1

58
57
55
54

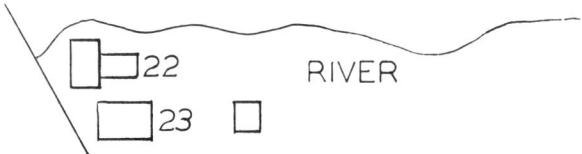
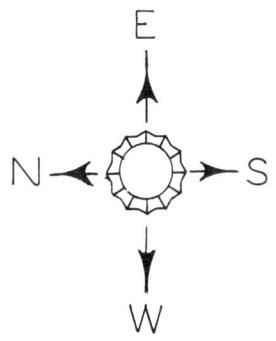
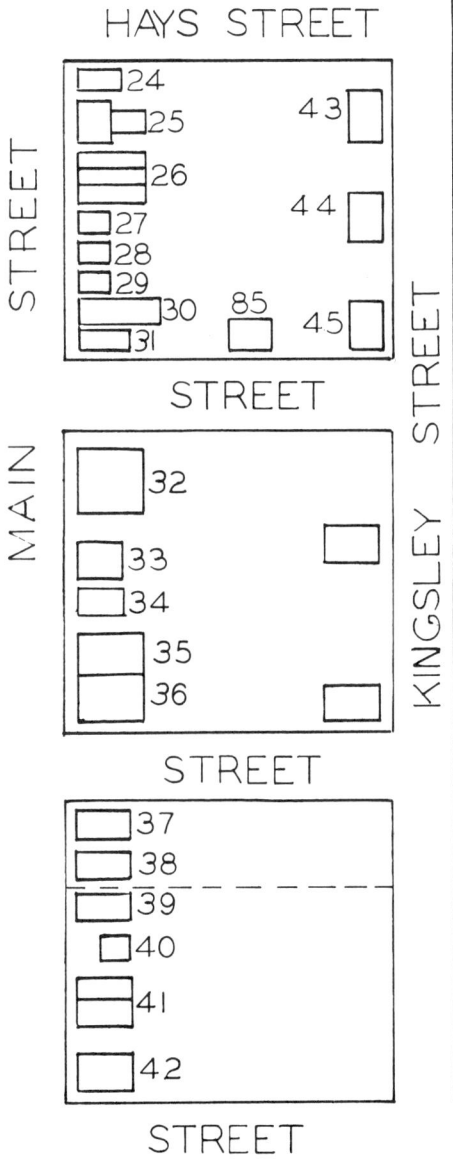
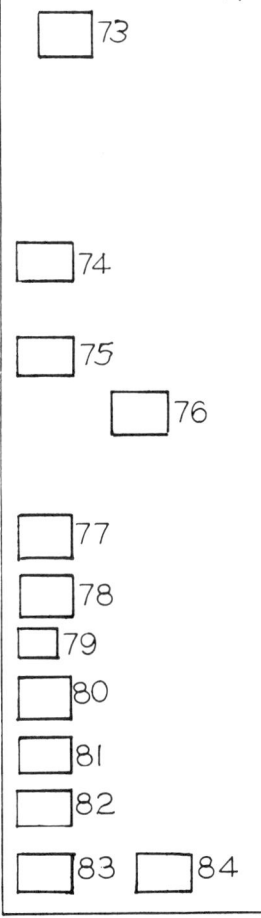
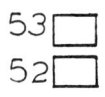

Directory
of
Residents for 1861

A special census in July of 1861 showed a Mono County population of 3,226. There were 1,985 at Aurora, 987 at Monoville, the remainder of 345 being spread in other parts of the County.[1] J. Wells Kelly's First Directory of Nevada Territory includes a list of over 570 Aurora residents. The Kelly list was compiled either in the fall of 1861 or early in 1862. Since Aurora was claimed by Mono County until the Boundary Survey of 1863, Kellys list forms much of what could be called a first directory of Mono County residents. Since the bulk of the population of Mono County was highly transient and since many at the mines were not citizens, the actual number of residents remains incomplete. Note, for example, that Kelly's Aurora list contains half the number reported in the summer census.

The following complements Kelly's Aurora list, and is drawn from three sources: a Monoville Poll List from the June 1st election of 1861 which contains 498 names; secondly, a poll list of 32 names taken at the August 20, 1861, election at Dotown; a third source, the "Minutes of the Monoville Union Club", kept by William C. Meredith and containing 143 names. In forming the following list I have numbered the names on the three lists and have included Kelly's since some names appear on more than one of the sources. A number 1 appearing after a name signifies the Monoville Poll List, a number 2 refers to the Dogtown list, a number 3 to that of the Monoville Union Club, and a number 4 appears if the name is in Kelly's Aurora list. The following may be considered a First Directory of Mono County Residents. Voting registers for the County of Mono form a record of residency, at least for those qualified to vote, for the years from 1870 to 1900. The Monoville Poll List, which was rescued from destruction in the Bridgeport Dump by the Webbs and W. Lee Symmonds, is written in an unusually illegible hand, the transcriber having relied heavily on his own system of phonetics.

236

A

Adams, John H., 1-3
Airs, Wm., 1
Alexander, John, 1
Alexander, S. H. P., 1
Anderson, John, 1

Aylard, James, 3
Allen, H. B., 1-4
Ault, G. S., 1-4
Anderson, Geo., 1

Anderson, Peter, 1-4
Andrews, J., 1
Anocia, J. B., 2
Arris, J. M., 1

B

B_____, Jas., 1
Baker, John, 2-4
Balinger, F. M., 1
Bangs, A. S., 3
Banister, J. A., 1-4
Baker, A. H., 1-4
Barker, Jas., 1-4
Barkley, Alex I., 3
Barsell, J. J., 1
Barrett, Thomas E., 2
Bastwick, J., 1
Batty, F., 1
Beach, C. C., 1
Beck, John, 1
Bedford, P. M., 1
Begole, C. D., 3
Bell, A. C., 3-4

Bell, J. H., 1
Bell, W. H., 1
Bennett, P., 1
Benter, Adam, 1
Berdsill, L., 1
Bevens, A., 1
Biderman, J. C., 1-2*
Bivens, Alexander, 3
Bixby, M., 1
Bland, J., 1
Boomershine, J., 1-3-4*
Boston, G. E., 1
Bowen, Thos. A., 1
Bowling, M. L., 1
Boynton, Wm., 1-3
Brady, B., 1
Brady, G., 1-4

Bradley, F., 1
Brandy, J., 1
Brant, A., 1
Brewer, W., 1
Brill, N., 1
Brock, S., 1
Brown, Chas., 1-4
Brown, John, 3-4
Brown, J. W. E., 1
Bryant, J. H., 1-3
Bryant, J. W., 1-3
Buckhart, F., 1
Bur_____, S. S., 1
Burton, Joseph, 3
Byrnes, E. C., 1
Byrnes, Jas., 1
Byrns, J., 1

C

Callen, Rbt., 1
Cameron, J., 1-3
Cammel, R. A., 1
Campbell, Peter, 1-3
Campbell, R. A., 3
Cane, Jno. W., 1
Carland, P. H., 1
Carter, J. L., 1-2
Carter, Sol., 1
Caven, Thos., 2
Cavenough, M., 1
Cavey, H., 1
Chambers, B., 1
Chandler, Stephen, 1-3
Chapman, L. B., 3
Chase, S. C., 3
Chauncy, John, 1
Chick, Geo. W., 1-2

Childs, J. A., 1-4
Childs, Robert H., 1-3
Clark, Henry, 3
Clark, J., 1
Clark, Lewis, 1-2
Cochrane, Thos., 1-4
Cofs, N., 1
Cofs, Wm., 1
Cole, J., 2-4
Coleman, A. C., 1
Coleman, H. M., 1
Colingwood, J., 1
Collen, Chris, 1
Colman, Asa, 3
Con___erton, John, 1
Connelly, A., 3
Conyer, Jno., 1
Cooley, J. S., 1

Cook, E. W., 1
Cook, Joseph S., 1-3
Coons, J., 1
Courling, Rbt., 1
Coulter, P., 1
Covall, W. W., 3
Cox, L. D., 1
Crabtree, W. C., 3
Cradelbaugh, A. C., 1
Craig, Fred W., 2-3
Craig, P. A., 3-4
Creague, P. A., 1
Crocker, A. W., 1
Cross, Wm., 3
Cupid, Wm., 1
Currins, Jas., 1
Curry, W., 1
Cutter, T. A., 1-4

D

Da___, L., 1
Dailey, D., 1
Dale, Mac., 1
Daley, C., 1
Daley, J. C., 1
Davidson, W., 1
Davis, B. K., 1
Davis, W. C., 1
Dawson, Wm., 1
Day, Lewis, 1
Day, Wm., 1
Dazel (Dalzell), John, 1

Dean, G. W., 1
Deblinger, C. P., 3
Derby, E., 1
Duchoo, Robt., 1
Duddles, Thos., 1
Dudley, John, 1
Dugdale, Thos., 1
Duncan, Jas., 1
Dunham, E. G., 1
Dunkin, G., 1-4
Dunlop, Wm., 1-4
Duval, M., 1

Desbrow, Wm., 1
Dobbins, Geo., 3
Dodge, E. G., 3
Dods, H. H., 1
Dods, J. F., 1
Donehugh, M., 1
Donnely, W., 1-4
Dority, Phil, 1
Downs, B. F., 1-2
Doyle, Jno., 1-4
Dryer, Ben., 1-4
Dryer, F., 1

237

*Mt. Biderman was named for this Bodie miner. Boomershine was involved in the Lundy discovery.

E

Edgerly, Frank, 1-3
Edwards, Wm. A., 1
Eliott, B., 1

Elly, J., 1
Elman, H., 1

English, Wm., 3
Esh, George, 1-3

F

Faning, Frederick, 2
Farland, H. L., 3
Farrote, G. S., 3
Farrote, I., 1-4
Farrow, John, 1
Felch, J. B., 1-3
Finney, J. F., (J. T.), 1*
Fletcher, F., 1

Flynn, Danl., 1
Foot, Geo., 1
Ford, John, 1
Fenter, W. D., 1-2
Fetzer, Fred, 3
Fine, J., 1
Finney, Geo. W., 3
Francis, D. G. (D. R.), 1*

Francis, James, 2
Freese, G. A., 1
Freidman, M., 1
French, Robert, 1
French, Samuel, 3-4
Fry., J. A., 1
Fud___, E. J., 1

*This may be the same Finney for whom Virginia City, Nevada, was named. Finney, known as Old Virginia, was reportedly killed June 20, 1861. Francis was one of the first officers of Mono County.

G

Garretson (Garrison), J. S., 3-4
Gelatt, J. W., 1
Gibbin, Jon., 1
Gilbert, Geo., 1
Gilholly, M., 1

Goldner, N., 1-4
Goodrich, A. C., 1-3
Goodrich, J., 1-2
Gorden, Jno., 1
Graves, J. E., 1

Gray, Saml., 1
Green, J. W., 1
Guile, Gideon, 3
Gunn, J. W., 3
Gunter, C., 1

H

H___, Samuel, 1
Hadereff, H., 1
Haggett, W., 1
Halpin, D., 1
Ham, G. A., 3
Hambridge, E., 1-3
Hamilton, L. W., 1
Hamilton, W. D., 1-4
Hancock, D., 1
Hanford, W. T., 1
Hanness, J., 1
Harder, J. R., 1
Harding, Issac, 1-3
Harrison, Albert, 1
Hart, L. F., 1
Harter, J. M., 1
Harvey, Robt., 1
Harwood, B. W., (D. W.), 1-3

Haseltine, T., 1
Haslen, James M., 1-3
Has___, Geo. A., 1
Hefner, J., 1
Henderson, D. M., 3
Henesy, D., 1
Henry, J., 1-4
Heuff (Huff), John W., 1-3
Hiatt, O. R., 3
Hicks, W. H., 1
Hiedly, N. G., 1
Hitchcock, A. H., 1-2
Hively (Hinley), W. S., 1-3
Holbrook, Eli., 1-3
Honnefs, James, 3
Hood, Samuel, 1
Hoopes, A., 1

Hopner, J. C., 1
Howard, J. B., 1
Howd, S., 1
Howeth, J. W., 1
Howser, Mich., 1-3
Hubbard, Clay, 1
Hubbs, J. R., 1
Hues (Hughes), L. E., 3
Hues, S. E., 1
Humphrey, D. R., 1
Hunt, Andrew, 3
Hurber, A., 1
Hutcherson, R., 1
Hutcherson, Wm., 1
Hutten, J. J., 1
Hyte, G. A., 1
Hyte, J., 1

I

Ingram, P., 1-4

J

James, W. B., 1
Jenkins, E. G., 1
Jewell, J. B., 1
Johnson, Jas., 1-3-4
Johnson, Wm., 1-2-4

Jones, A. E., 1
Jones, B. J., 1
Jones, D. A., 1
Jones, D. E., 1

Jones, J. R., 1
Jones, S., 1
Jones, S., 1-4
Joslyn, S. C., 3

K

Keating, R., 1
Keelan (Keefer), Jas., 1-4
Keer, Jas., 1
Kempton, S. S., 1
Kellog, W. R., 1-4
Kelly, M., 1
Kelper, S. P., 1

Kenny, J., 1
Kepear, Cha., 3
Kearn, Jno., 1
Kief, T., 1
Kiethly, H. C., 1
King, A., 1
King, Ed., 1

King, G. W., 1
King, H. G., 1
Kirkpatrick, I., 1
Kirney, M., 1
Knox, John, G., 3
Koerber, F. P., 3

238

L

Lagendorf, E. I., 3
Lane, Samuel, 1-3
Laroo (La Rue), J., 1-4
Laucet, Wm., 3
Laurence, J., 1
Leach, O. G., 1
Levey, L., 1
Lundy, N. J., 1

Lyott (Luckett), Jno., 1
Libbeey, John G., 1-3
Lochr, Tho. H., 3
Long, Chris., 1
Low, B., 1
Luce, West, 2
Luckett, A. W., 1

Lynch, Jas., 1
Lynch, M., 1
Lynch, S. A., 1-3
Lyon, Rbt., 1
Lyons, G. D., 1
Lyons, Jas., 1-4
Lynnerote, John, 3

M

McAlister, S., 1
McAllen, D. W., 1
McAmally, F., 1
McAphee, Robt., 1
McCabe, Jno., 1
McCann, Hamilton, 3
McCarther, J. S., 1
McCon——lea, S., 1
McCormick, J. M., 1
McCully, M., 1
McCurdy, Wm., 3
McDonald, J. C., 1-4
McEvoy, M. C., 1
McGaffey, H. A., 1-3
McGaffey, W. H., 1-3
McGee, S. L., 1
McGee, Thos., 1*
McGerry, A., 1
McCrane, Thos., 1
McGiff, T., 1
McIntosh, J. B., 3
McKay, Robert, 2
McKinney, B. F., 1

McKinsey, A., 1

McLaughlin, Tho., 3-4
McMahan (McMann), J., 1-4
McRoberts, L., 1
McWharter, J. B., 1
Machin, T. M., 3*
Mahoney, Wm., 1
Malcom, L., 1
Man, C. L., 1
Man, Milton, 1
Mann, A. P., 1-3
Markle, John, 3
Marks, L. N., 1
Martin, W. M., 1
Mason, ——, S., 1
Masters, J. D., 1
Me, R. L., 1
Means, J. L., 2
Meek, E. E., 1-4
Mehr., L. F., 1-3
Meiggs, M. B., 1
Meredith, William C., 1-3*

Merriam, R., 1
Meyers, D. H., 1
Miles, C. F., 1-3
Miligan, Wm., 1
Miller, S. M., 1
Miller, Thos., 1
Mills, C. W., 1*
Mills, Samuel, 1
Mitchell, A. H., 1-3*
Moorman, Thomas Jefferson, 3*
Moore, H. E., 1
Moore, John T., 1
Morgan, Jos., 3
Morrison, H., 1
Morrison, J. A., 1-3
Morrison, Joseph, 1-3-4
Muckford, J., 1
Mulhern, Chas. P., 1
Mulin, F., 1
Munrow, M. E., 1-3
Murray, Chas., 1
Murry, Jas., 1-4

N

Nelson, Charles, 1
Nichols, A., 1
Nolan, L., 1

Norris, Martin, 1-3
Norst, C., 1*

Norton, W., 1
Nye, Peter, 3*

O

O'Neal, R. C., 1
O'Rook, Thomas, S., 1

Olds, L. M., 1
Olt, F., 1

Ort, H., 1

*The McGee family was among the first to arrive at the diggings, having driven cattle through Owens Valley. McGee Creek bears the family name. Machin was later lieutenant governor of California. Meredith was leader of the patriotic Monoville Union Club. Another Meredith, James M., may have been related to the above. James crossed the plains from Penn. in 1849, returned after two years, crossed overland again in 1852 and was at Monoville in 1860. He died in Aurora in 1882. Mills died in one of his own buildings on Mills Street in Bodie in 1883. Mitchell was involved in the Owens Valley Indian War. Moorman is the namesake of Morman Meadows, which came to its present misspelling as a result of more recent mapmaking. As late as 1883, the Moorman spelling was preserved in Bodie papers. In 1882, the North Carolina native was a miner aged 70 at Tioga District. He is undoubtedly related to a Moorman who crossed overland in 1849. Norst, self-proclaimed discoverer of Dogtown and Monoville. Nye was reported to have been a brother of Governor Nye of Nevada. Quint was involved in the so called election fraud. Richter was namesake of the Richter mining ground at Bodie.

P

Palmer, Wm., 1
Pan___re___s, E., 1
Parker, A. P., 1-3
Parker, P. G., 1
Parker, William, 1-3
Parmler, D. J., 1
Parsons, Cha. A., 3
Patten, J. M., 1
Patterson, J. H., 1
Patterson, R. S., 1-3-4

Patton, J. E., 1-3
Pearson, A., 1
Pellinger, J. G., 1
Perry, L. E., 3
Peterman, J. G., 1
Peterson, Chas., 1
Peyett, O. B., 1
Phillips, J. H., 1
Phillips, Nathan, 1-3
Philpen, T., 1

Philson, J., 1
Pierce, D. B., 3
Pierce, James, 2-4
Pierce, L., 1
Pope, H. S., 1
Pope, Wm., 1
Ponasky, Newman, 1
Preble, Charles, 1-3
Putnam, O., 1

Q

Quint, L., 1*

Quail, W. H., 1

R

Ramsdell, A., 1
Reed, J. M., 1
Reed, Jas., 1
Reed, P., 1-3-4
Rice, J. W., 3
Rice, John, 1
Richie (Ritchie), W. A., 1
Richter, John, 2*
Riley, C. P., 1
Riley, D., 1
Riley, John, 1

Ripley, C. J., 1
Roberson, F., 1
Roberson, L. T., 1
Roberson, N., 1
Robertson, L. M., 3
Robinson, H. F., 3
Roderbank, J. W., 1-4
Roderfer, D., 1
Rogers, A., 1
Rogers, Albt., 1
Rogers, J. J., 1

Roland, J. M., 1
Romeo, Paul, 1
Rop, H., 1
Ross, J., 1
Rothchilds, B., 1-3
Rothermill, J., 1
Rush, J. G., 1
Russell, A., 1
Russell, David, 3
Russell, J. P., 1
Ryan, Michael, 1-2

S

Sabin, Chas., 1
Safford, W., 3
Safron, M., 1
Sandar, F., 1
Sanders, J. B., 1
Sands, Wm. W., 1
Savage, E. H., 1
Sawn, Leroy, 3
Saxon, Leeroy, 1
Schore___, H. C., 3
Scott, D. W., 1
Sewell, F., 2
Sewell, T., 1
Shafner, L., 1
Shaw, J. R., 1-3
Shephard, Geo., 1
Sherman, Issac H., 3
Sherman, J. H., 1
Sherrell, Jas., 1

Sherrill, Saml., 1
Shilling, Jake D., 3
Shreves, John A., 1-3
Sill, H. C., 1
Simpson, Saml., 1
Sinnamon, Jas., 1-3*
Slutter, E., 1
Smith, Chas. E., 1-4
Smith, G., 1
Smith, J. R., 1
Smith, Jno., 1
Smith, R., 1
Smith, W. J., 1
Smoot, Minor B., 1
Snowe, Geo., 1
Spawutilus, F. W., 3
Spencer, ___W., 1
Spencer, E., 1
Springer, J., 1

Stacks, Geo., 1*
Starr, A. C., 1-3
Stearns, W. H., 3
Stebbins, I. P., 3
Stebins, J. B., 1
Stedam, F. E., 1
Stephens, Issac., A., 2
Sterne, J. A., 1
Stewart, S., 1
Stewart, Wm., 1
Stoddart, Thos. Robertson, 3
Strat___, E. W., 2
Stull, S., 1
Sullivan, M., 1
Sullivan, P., 1
Summers, John, 1-2-4
Swimming, John, 1
Swimming, Jos., 1
Switzer, Gandlip, 2

T

Taylor, F. P., (P.B.), 3
Thatcher, A. M., 1-4
Thomas, J., 1
Thompson, Andrew, 3
Thompson, J. C., 3
Thompson, J. H., 1

Thompson, R., 1
Thorp, G. B., 1
Till, R., 1
Tilton, S. S., 1-4*
Timmonds, J. T., 1-3
Travis, D. C., 3

Trowsdel, J. H., 1
Tucker, J., 1
Turner, A. B., 1
Turner, J. B., 1
Turner, Samuel, 1
Tyler, H., 1-4

*Stacks was possibly a husband of Adaline Carson. Sinnamon and Tilton are both remembered in place names, the Sinnamon Cut and Sinnamon Meadows, and Tilton Lake. Vining reportedly moved on to Aurora where he died.

*Whitney, one of the first to locate at Bridgeport Valley, was also one of the first at the Comstock Lode, his name appearing on a list of first locators.

241

Bibliography

Bancroft, Hubert Howe, *California Inter Pocula.* The History Company, San Francisco, 1890.

Bancroft, Hubert Howe, *Register of Pioneer Inhabitants of California, 1842-1848.* Los Angeles, Dawson's Book Shop, 1964.

Bancroft Scraps. (A scrapbook of California County items), Bancroft Library.

Bidwell, John, "The First Emigrant Train to California", *The Century Magazine,* Vol. XLI, Nov. 1890.

Brewer, William H., *Up And Down California in 1860-1864.* University of California Press, Berkeley, 1949.

Browne, J. Ross, *Mining Adventures.* Paisano Press, Balboa Island, Calif., 1961.

Browne, J. Ross, *Resources of the Pacific Slope.* D. Appleton & Co., New York, 1869.

Buckbee, Edna Bryan, *Saga of Old Tuolumne.* The Press of The Pioneers, Inc., New York, 1935.

Bunnell, L. H., *Discovery of the Yosemite.* G. W. Gerlicher, Los Angeles, 1911.

Cain, Ella, *The Story of Bodie.* Fearon Publishers, San Francisco, 1956.

Cain, Ella, *The Story of Early Mono County.* Fearon Publishers, Inc., San Francisco, 1961.

Chalfant, W. A., *The Story of Inyo.* W. A. Chalfant, 1922.

Clemens, Samuel, *Roughing It.* Harper and Brothers, New York, 1904.

Colcord, R. K., *"Reminiscences of Life in Territorial Nevada",* California Historical Quarterly, Vol. VII, No. 2, June, 1928.

Coy, Owen C., *California County Boundaries.* California Historical Survey Commission, Berkeley, 1923.

Danberg, Grace, *Carson Valley Days.* The Carson Valley Historical Society, 1972.

Davis, Winfield J., *History of Political Conventions in California 1849-1892.* Sacramento, 1893.

De Groot, Henry, *Sketches of the Washoe Silver Mines.* Hutchings & Rosenfield, San Francisco, 1860. (Reprinted in the Talisman Press edition of *The First Directory of Nevada Territory,* Los Gatos, 1962).

De Quille, Dan, *The Big Bonanza.* Alfred A. Knofp, New York, 1964.

Ewers, John C., Ed., *Adventures of Zenas Leonard, Fur Trader.* University of Oklahoma Press, 1959.

Fremont, John Charles, *Memoirs of My Life.* Belford, Clarke & Co., New York, 1887.

Fremont, John Charles, Allan Nevins, Ed., *Narratives of Exploration and Adventure.* Longmans, Green & Co., New York, 1956.

Frickstad, Walter, *A Century of California Postoffices, 1849-1954.* Pacific Rota Printing Co., Oakland, 1955.

Great Register of Mono County. Voting registers for the years 1871, 1872, 1873, 1875, 1877, 1879, 1880, 1882, 1886, 1898.

Gudde, Erwin, *California Place Names.* University of California Press, Berkeley, 1960.

Hamblet, Millie Hunewill, *Saga of the Circle H.* 1961.

Haskins, C. W., *Argonauts of California.* Fords, Howard & Hulbert, New York, 1890.

Hinkle, George and Bliss, *Sierra-Nevada Lakes.* The Bobbs-Merrill Co., Inc., 1949.

Jackson, W. Turentine, Ed., *Twenty Years on the Pacific Slope.* (Letters of Henry Eno from California and Nevada, 1848-1871), Yale University Press, 1965.

Kelly, J. Wells, *First Directory of Nevada Territory.* Talisman Press, Los Gatos, 1962.

King, Clarence, Francis Farquhar, Ed., *Mountaineering in the Sierra Nevada.* W. W. Norton & Co. Inc., New York, 1935.

Le Conte, Joseph, *A Journal of Ramblings Through The High Sierra of California.* The Sierra Club, San Francisco, 1960.

Lyman, George, *The Saga of The Comstock Lode.* Scribners, New York, 1934.

McIntosh, F. W., *Mono County,* 1908.

Muir, John, *The Mountains of California.* Doubleday & Co., Inc., New York, 1961.

Russell, Carl P., *"Early Mining Excitements East of Yosemite".* Sierra Club Bulletin Reprint, 1928.

Russell, Carl P., *One Hundred Years in Yosemite.* University of California Press, Berkeley, 1947.

Scenes of Wonder and Curiosity From Hutchings' California Magazine, 1856-1861. R. R. Olmstead, Ed., Howell-North, Berkeley, 1962.

Scrugham, James, Ed., *Nevada, A Narrative of the Conquest of a Frontier Land.* The American Historical Society, Inc., New York, 1935.

Sherman, Edwin, *Fifty Years of Masonry in California.* George Spaulding & Co., San Francisco, 1898.

Thompson & West, *History of Nevada.* Howell-North, Berkeley, 1958.

Tobie, Harvey, *No Man Like Joe.* Binfords & Mort, Portland, Ore., 1949.

Treadwell, Edward, *The Cattle King.* The Christopher Publishing House, Boston, 1950.

Trexler, Keith, *The Tioga Road.*

Wasson, Joseph, *Bodie and Esmeralda.* Spaulding, Barto & Co., San Francisco, 1878.

Wasson, Joseph, *Complete Guide to the Mono County Mines.* 1879.

Wedertz, Clarence R., *Journals, 1890's-1900's.* Unpublished.

Wedertz, Frank S., *Bodie: 1859-1900.* Chalfant Press, 1969.

Whitney, H. A., *"Mineral Resources of Mono County", Report of The State Mineralogist, 1888.* State Printing Office, Sacramento.

Newspapers:

Alpine Chronicle	*Bridgeport Union*
Bodie Daily Standard	*Esmeralda Union*
Bodie Evening Miner	*Mariposa Gazette*
Bodie Free Press	*Mono-Alpine Chronicle*
Bodie Weekly Standard-News	*Reno Evening Gazette*
Bridgeport Chronicle-Union	*Territorial Enterprise*
	Visalia Weekly Delta

Records:

Mono County Assessor's Records: Plat Maps, assessor's maps and descriptions, inventories.

Mono County Clerk's Records: Mining and Real Estate Deeds, mining districts record books, Minute Books of The Board of Supervisors, miscellaneous records.

Mono County Sheriff and Tax Collector: Sheriff's Record books, and various tax and sheriff records and sale listings (quite a number of old Mono County record books held privately).

245

INDEX
For Additional Surnames See Appendix

C

D